THE LAWS OF LINKEDIN

23 LAWS TO ATTRACT YOUR
IDEAL CLIENTS, BUILD A LOYAL
FOLLOWING, AND SCALE YOUR
INCOME TO SEVEN-FIGURES
ON LINKEDIN

CULLEN P. HAYNES

BALBOA.PRESS
A DIVISION OF HAY HOUSE

Copyright © 2024 Cullen P. Haynes.

All rights reserved. No part of this book may be used or reproduced by any means, graphic, electronic, or mechanical, including photocopying, recording, taping or by any information storage retrieval system without the written permission of the author except in the case of brief quotations embodied in critical articles and reviews.

Balboa Press books may be ordered through booksellers or by contacting:

Balboa Press
A Division of Hay House
1663 Liberty Drive
Bloomington, IN 47403
www.balboapress.com.au
AU TFN: 1 800 844 925 (Toll Free inside Australia)
AU Local: (02) 8310 7086 (+61 2 8310 7086 from outside Australia)

Because of the dynamic nature of the Internet, any web addresses or links contained in this book may have changed since publication and may no longer be valid. The views expressed in this work are solely those of the author and do not necessarily reflect the views of the publisher, and the publisher hereby disclaims any responsibility for them.

The author of this book does not dispense medical advice or prescribe the use of any technique as a form of treatment for physical, emotional, or medical problems without the advice of a physician, either directly or indirectly. The intent of the author is only to offer information of a general nature to help you in your quest for emotional and spiritual well-being. In the event you use any of the information in this book for yourself, which is your constitutional right, the author and the publisher assume no responsibility for your actions.

Any people depicted in stock imagery provided by Getty Images are models, and such images are being used for illustrative purposes only. Certain stock imagery © Getty Images.

Print information available on the last page.

ISBN: 979-8-7652-0107-7 (sc)
ISBN: 979-8-7652-0085-8 (e)

Balboa Press rev. date: 11/08/2024

Praise for *The Laws of LinkedIn*

Cullen's boundless energy and incredible achievements leap off every page. This book is a testament to his remarkable spirit and relentless drive!

Hayder Shkara

Principal, Justice Family Lawyers | Olympian, Taekwondo

'The Laws of LinkedIn' is a game-changing guide that offers practical, proven strategies for mastering the platform. Cullen Haynes shares his hard-earned wisdom to help you attract clients and scale your success.

Reena Strehle

LinkedIn Top 250 Influencer | Top 100 Thought Leader of the Year

In this brilliant volume you will find out all you need to know to make LinkedIn work for you. You will be entertained and educated, and end up with keys to success on this effective medium. And perhaps most fun in the reading is making a new friend, Cullen Haynes, entertaining, always interesting, and loyal to you.

Charles Lowenhaupt

Best-Selling Author of *Freedom from Wealth & The Chase Continues* | Lawyer | Chairman & Partner, Lowenhaupt & Chasnoff LLC

Cullen was a magician, always spreading his magic dust. Not only is he a LinkedIn entrepreneur with a story to tell but a man who listens and supports those singing from the same song book. Decent, clever, and affable—the Houdini of our time.

Darren Mort

Best-Selling Author of *Isla's Song* | Barrister | Mediator | Director

An essential read for professionals in law, accounting, engineering, and other services looking to expand their networks and accelerate practice growth. This book offers actionable strategies and insights to help you cultivate meaningful relationships that drive business success.

Alistair Marshall
Best-Selling Author of *Grow Your Professional Services Practice* | Director of Professional Services BD

Cullen Haynes' book is a game-changer for mastering LinkedIn. With his vast knowledge and impressive following, he provides invaluable insights that will truly elevate your online presence and change your business forever.

Domenic Nesci
Best-Selling Author of *You Won't F*ck It Up: Buying Property is Easier Than You Think*

'The Laws of the LinkedIn' is a fascinating read. Cullen Haynes has achieved great success from his prolific use of the app. These are the laws he divined from his own first-hand experience.

Peter Hunt
Author of *The Arched Eyebrow Review* | Top Tier Law Partner | Mediator

Cullen is a LinkedIn genius! The Laws of LinkedIn reveals his best-kept secrets, empowering professionals to leverage the platform to significantly boost their business success.

David Gale
Director & Family Lawyer, Gale Family Law | TikTok Celebrity

Cullen Haynes is an inspiring and dynamic leader who played a pivotal role in getting me into LinkedIn. I remember opening my feed and seeing this guy consistently sharing valuable tips, generating massive engagement, and leaving a real impact. That sparked my own journey, and here we are today. Cullen's book is packed with the same wisdom and energy that first drew me in—you're going to love it!

Edward Zia
LinkedIn Certified Consultant

Cullen's insights in The Laws of LinkedIn are game-changing for anyone looking to elevate their networking game. His advice always cuts through the noise.

Stefanie Costi
LinkedIn Top Voice | The Anti-Bullying Lawyer

Cullen is a powerhouse of Australian LinkedIn. His prominence, generosity, and forward-thinking approach have enabled him to serve a great number of Australian lawyers. Any insights he has to share about how he built his brand (and the book of business that no doubt travels with it!) are well worth reading.

James d'Apice
Founder, Gravamen Law | Coffee and a Case Note Series

Rarely do we hear professional (and personal) wisdom from a value-driven author who lives and breathes their wisdom, with their words leaping off the page into our learning. Good onya Cullen Haynes.

Bill Ash
Best-Selling Author of *Redesigning Conversations* | Lawyer | Coach

Cullen is pure positive energy. And this attitude flows into all he does and impacts all those around him. His insights are reflective of his l passion for learning and knowledge. Cullen is one of those rare individuals who leaves people and situations better than he found them

Perpetua 'Pepe' Kish
Founder & Director, Balance Family Law | Award-Winning Lawyer

The Laws of LinkedIn cracks the code to online networking, turning connections into opportunities. Packed with tips, it's your shortcut to LinkedIn mastery and business growth!

Dino Pacella
LinkedIn Legend | Founder of National Finance Brokers Day | Head of Marketplace Finance

For Emmy, Benji, Lachie, & Alfie. My foundation, my purpose, and my greatest loves. This book is for you, always.

With all my heart,

Cullen

Contents

Everyone Has a Story xiii
PROLOGUE xv
23 Laws Preface – What This Book Is About (And What It's Not About) xxi
A WARNING to the Reader xxvii

Law #0 - Discover Your Tribe 1
Law #1 - Just Start 10
Law #2 - There's No Limit: Post Now, Post Often 17
Law #3 - LinkedIn is Not a Resume: See & Be Seen 23
Law #4 - Repetition & Consistency are Key 🔑 41
Law #5 – ABC: Always Be Connecting 48
Law #6 – Celebrate Good Times, Come On! 57
Law #7 – Leave a Message, After the Tone 67
Law #8 – Start an Entourage: Turn on Creator Mode 78
Law #9 – The 80/20 Rule of Sales (And Life) 85
Law #10 – Follow Me: Like, Share & Subscribe 95
Law #11 – The Magic of Seven Likes: Building Bonds That Matter 101
Law #12 – The Reciprocity Effect: Building Relationships Through Recommendations 107
Law #13 – Love yourself first ♡ 115
Law #14 – Engage or Fade: The Impact of Commenting on LinkedIn 122
Law #15 - The Gift of Connection: Leverage Birthdays to Deepen Bonds 128
Law #16 – Elevate and Celebrate: The Art of Acknowledging Achievements 135
Law #17 – Video Killed the Article Star: Why Video Wins 143

Law #18 – Document, Don't Create: Business Is Personal 155

Law #19 – Polls of Persuasion: The Yes/No Paradigm 163

Law #20 – Circulate to Percolate: Elevate Others Above Yourself .. 176

Law #21 – Pay It Forward: The Rule of Reciprocity: Elevate Your Influence by Connecting Others 191

Law #22 – Book Yourself Solid & Command the Clock: Make Yourself Invaluable by Controlling Access 202

Law #23 – Mobilize Your Tribe: Harness the Strength of Networking Groups 218

Bonus Law - The Ultimate Goal: Take Your Online Interactions Offline 227

EPILOGUE 231

Some Final Thoughts to Help You Win Big on LinkedIn 233

ACKNOWLEDGMENTS 243

Everyone Has a Story

If one advances confidently in the direction of their dreams, and endeavors to live the life which they have imagined, they will meet with a success unexpected in common hours.
— Henry David Thoreau

My path to LinkedIn success is anything but conventional.

I wasn't born into wealth, and I didn't attend a prestigious private school. I'm just a country kid from Albury–Wodonga. In my relatively short life, I've navigated through more careers than most people might in a lifetime.

It all began with a job at Big W in Albury during my teenage years. Later, I became school captain at Xavier High School. Went to University. I worked as a professional magician to pay my way through. Loved it. Earned a degree in radiography. Hated it. That led me to pivot again, landing a role as a Guest Experience manager in hotels looking after VVIP clients like John Cleese, Oprah, Lady Gaga, and Bon Jovi and many more. Eventually, I pursued my MBA, then moved to Macquarie Bank. After two years there, I ventured into entrepreneurship, starting a mortgage broking business with one other person. Over six years, we scale to a team of 18, served thousands of lawyers, earned numerous awards, and I was recognized as the #3 Broker out of 19,000 in Australia. And it all started with LinkedIn.

Our biggest challenge when launching the business? Obscurity. *"People won't flow you until they know you,"* as Grant Cardone said. LinkedIn allowed us to overcome that, for free (other than time invested). It allowed us to create, curate and put out valuable content and say *"Hey world, we're here. Deal with us!."* LinkedIn taught us that we had a voice worth listening to, and our tribe would not only find us but value us as well.

What advice would I give to someone starting (or restarting) on LinkedIn today? There's no one else in the world like you - no one with your rich and storied history and unique journey. That's your edge. For me, no one else has had the eclectic career path I've walked. No one I know had a Mother & Father who gave them Tony Robbins & Jim Rohn tapes (yes cassette tapes) in primary school; fostering a lifelong passion for learning & self-enrichment (you'll see this throughout the book). No one in my industry has the attention to detail, I needed in order to learn anatomy. And I bet no one else has X-Rayed a person with a samurai sword through their stomach, nor got to know the wonderful and interesting things that can find their way into the human body; I'll say no more. No one else has had their customer services skills sharpened to the point where they can think on their feet and look after very high expectation guests in hotels; the kind that only wanted 6 raisins in their morning oats (true story). No one else has worked at Macquarie Bank in the way I did helping clients, through vehicle finance, putting dreams in their driveways. And no one else had a tech-savvy wife like mine, who's a wizard (or Witch) with Final Cut Pro and MacBook's, levelling up my digital game.

This unique blend of experiences is what Scott Adams the author of *Dilbert*, calls your **persuasion stack** - all the life experience and lessons that combine, compound, and work in concert to make you lethal in what you do.

So go out there, embrace and lean into your own persuasion stack, be authentically you and make it count.

— CPH

PROLOGUE

*It's not about being better than anyone else, but
better than who you were yesterday.*
— *Wayne Dyer*

Dear Reader.

If you've picked up this book, I believe you're a lot like me—empowered, hungry and fully aware that if you're going to make things happen in this life, it's on you. You're not waiting for someone else to grant you success. You're out there, *making it happen.*

If you're like me, you've had your fair share of *"no's"* and *"you can't do that."* And also like me, because of your passion and enthusiasm, you've ignored them all and said simply, *"Challenge Accepted!."*

Enthusiasm comes from the word *"enthousiasmos,"* which means *inspired by a divine spirit or the Gods.* It's a sense of being driven by something bigger than yourself – where your energy is fuelled by a higher source, sparking creativity and motivation. When you're enthusiastic, it doesn't just push you to be great in your field; it drives you to continually evolve into the best version of yourself. That fire inside, that passion – it really does feel like magic, propelling you forward every single day.

This idea aligns with the Japanese concept of **Kaizen**, which translates to *"continuous improvement"* a concept that's deeply engrained at Legal Home Loans. Kaizen teaches us that small, incremental improvements over time lead to profound transformation. Whether in business, life or your personal growth, the power lies in making consistent, daily progress. Enthusiasm fuels this process, turning each major victory into a stepping stone toward excellence. Like Kaizen, it's about the pursuit of betterment – not overnight, but through sustained effort and passion over the long term.

As a former physics major, I'm a big believer in quantum physics and the multiverse. For every decision you make – whether big or small - there's an alternative reality where a different version of you lives out the other possibility. So, when I've faced resistance or feedback, I remind myself, that somewhere, there's another "me" living a completely different life – maybe better, maybe worse, but always different.

You see, for every major event in my life, I've had people tell me that I can't do something or try and hold me back. They've told me to tone it down, slow down, to take it easy. My university professor once called me a maniac. Friends in school said I was destined for fame – either for something brilliant or utterly foolish. And the harshest words often come from those who love you the most. They'll clap back these 4 words *"you can't do that"* veiled as love and care, not because they doubt your abilities, but because they fear seeing you fail or get hurt.

I was once told, *"You'll never afford to move to Sydney."* I moved here when I was 18 with enough money to put a deposit bond on a rental and buy some furniture and appliances.

I was told, *"You'll never work as a croupier - you're colourblind."* Instead, I was offered a job in hotels that the very same day, a role that would lead me to meet my future business partner, Andrew Johnson.

I was told, *"You'll never finish an MBA in 2 years while working full time."* I completed mine in 1.5 years, the same year I married the love of my life.

I was told, *"You'll never get a role at Macquarie Group with no banking experience. And no one passes their psychometric test."* I passed on my first try and landed the role after my second interview.

I was told, *"You know Cullen, most brokers fail in their first 6 months."* I've reached #3 in the country, leading a team of 18 at our company, Legal Home Loans. And for the record, whenever someone starts a sentence with *"You know…"* I usually tune out (and you should too).

I was once told, *"You'll never afford a house in Sydney, let alone an apartment."* Today, I live in my dream home on the Northern Beaches with my beautiful wife, two sons, and a Labradoodle called Alfie.

I was told, *"You're too young to partner with the Law Society of NSW,"* a prestigious member body for lawyers in Australia. Not only did we partner with them, but we've also formed relationships with nearly every major law society and bar association across Australia along with over 30% of Big Law firms partnered through our Staff Benefits Program.

I was told *"You can't start a business when no one knows you, you have no capital and you ain't got no contacts."* I'm particularly proud of my response to this taunt. I successfully answered it by mastering LinkedIn, through years of toil, devotion and simple trial and error.

What I've learned, dear reader, is that most feedback – outside of what comes from your loved ones – comes from other people's insecurities and neurosis. It's often more a reflection of them than you. For instance, when I announced to my colleagues I would be pursuing broking, their reply was one of doubt. When I pressed them how they knew that most brokers failed, I found that most of my critics had never actually been brokers themselves. So, here's a rule from my favourite Sufi poet, Rumi: **"When setting out on a journey do not seek advice from someone who never left home."**

These *"petty tyrants,"* as Wayne Dyer calls them, are few in number – maybe five or six in the world - but they tend to move around a lot. What I can tell you—hand on heart—is that this book contains everything I've learned from years of real-world experience; distilling all the secrets I know. This is not some LinkedIn guide for dummies written by an academic or random business author. These laws are raw, tested and they *work*. I've split-tested them many times, and I know they'll yield results for you just like they did for me.

These Laws form the foundation and have been crafted to be pragmatic, intuitive, and easy to apply. Inspired by Ryan Holiday, who highlights in *Perennial Seller* that most business books fail by not being either entertaining or practical, I've made it my mission to be both.

But here's a warning: This book isn't a *magic bullet*. You won't get results by applying these Laws just once. Consistency is key. Like Hal Elrod's *Miracle Equation*, all I ask is that you bring *"unwavering faith combined with extraordinary effort,"* which will help you achieve outstanding results that may seem like miracles.

Thank you for putting your faith in me, because I, dear reader, have faith in you. I'll never tell you that you can't do something or that it's impossible. In fact, I'll remind you that the word itself says: ***I'm***

Possible. Go ahead and build your castle with the bricks others throw at you.

If you're like me, you're charting your own course. I'm grateful that you've trusted this book to help you navigate not only LinkedIn but your entire professional life.

So, begin with the end in mind, enjoy the journey, and make it count.

From your friend and advocate,

Cullen

P.S. Be sure to connect with me on LinkedIn! https://www.linkedin.com/in/cullen-p-haynes/

23 Laws Preface – What This Book Is About (And What It's Not About)

This book is NOT about crafting the perfect LinkedIn page for beginners. Yet *The Laws of LinkedIn* will show you how to attract exponentially MORE dream clients than ever before.

This book is NOT about maximising eyeballs on your content. However, these Laws will ensure MORE *qualified members* of your tribe will be seeking you out for your services or offerings.

If you're struggling to gain traction on LinkedIn – whether it's connecting with clients or converting those that do connect—you may think your profile or content is to blame. More often than not, it's a *strategy and execution problem*. No one has provided you with a step-by-step guide to what works (and why) and how to build consistent growth when you gain traction.

Now, here's the thing—I'm not a LinkedIn coach or some self-proclaimed guru *this is about practical wisdom for your business and brand*. I've used these laws to grow a real business, not just gain followers. What I'm sharing here isn't theory, and it's definitely not some fluff designed to fill up a seminar or line the pockets of so-called *"experts."* These are raw, real, and hard-earned nuggets of wisdom that come from building a business from the ground up. If you're looking for practical advice that gets results, you're in the right place.

Too often, people are fed advice from marketing gurus about maintaining a strict content quote on LinkedIn – such as limiting your posts to a few pieces a week. I'm here to tell you that this advice is rhubarb, lies and false propaganda. In short, complete nonsense. If you're consistently posting *quality content* and adding real value to your tribe, you can post as often as you want. And guess what? You can offer your Call-To-Action (CTA) for your services more frequently as well.

A lawyer, one of my ideal clients, told me she was limiting herself to one or two posts a week for fear of annoying her network or diluting attention. I told her bluntly that she was mistaken, and this approach may not yield the desired results. I post *4-5 times a day.* My strategy involved frequent posting to increase visibility and engagement; thus resulting in new and repeat business. When she changed her mindset, her LinkedIn engagements and bookings skyrocketed, and I know yours will too.

Omnipresence should be your strategy, executed with this goal in mind. As Grant Cardone aptly puts it *"If you're not first, you're last."* Harsh, but true. You have the opportunity to leverage these insights to ensure your tribe knows what you do, so when they need your service, *you're* the first person that comes to mind. We've all been at a BBQ where someone casually mentions buying a product or service you offer—from someone else. Ouch! That stomach-turning feeling happens because you know your offering is superior, and they should have come to you. But here's the hard truth: it's not their fault. It's *yours* for not putting yourself out there enough so they know what you do.

This book will take you on the same journey I embarked on when Andrew & I launched Legal Home Loans. We've since built a strong, recognizable national brand across multiple channels, and a large part of that success is thanks to our General Manager and Marketing Maven, Aylin Unsal. Her strategic insight has allowed us to expand our presence beyond LinkedIn to various platforms. However, LinkedIn has always been our launch pad and daily staple, and the core principles that helped us build momentum and influence on this platform remain fundamental to everything we do today.

The Laws of LinkedIn are not just theories plucked from thin air they are proven tactics—they're the very strategies that helped us grow from a small team to Australia's #1 broker for lawyers. We continue to use these laws to this day, not just because they work, but because they've shaped how we think about influence, connection, and growth in our business. So, whether you're starting out or looking to take your LinkedIn presence to the next level, these laws are your blueprint for turning LinkedIn into your personal powerhouse.

By following these laws, you'll open the floodgates on every level of your LinkedIn presence—from follower count to engagement to being booked solid (even having a wait list) of your dream clients wanting to talk with a trusted expert. Wanting to talk with you.

Once you master the foundational laws introduced early in this book, we'll explore how to use them together to elevate your persuasion skills to what I call *weapons grade*. In essence, these laws are *Weapons of Mass Persuasion*. This book equips you with powerful persuasion strategies for maximum tribe engagement.

When you implement these laws, your LinkedIn presence will transform from a bland, two-dimensional resume into a dynamic, value-driven influence engine that helps you stand above your competition. You'll acquire an *unlimited* number of new clients, make more money for your invested time, and—most importantly—serve as many people as humanly possible, touching countless lives along the way.

THAT is what this book is about.

The LinkedIn Algorithm Myth

When it comes to the LinkedIn algorithm, many claim to have cracked the code, but the truth is, no one fully understands it. Anyone who says they have inside knowledge of how it works—much like with YouTube's algorithm— is often overselling their knowledge.

LinkedIn's algorithm, like other social media platforms, is a complex and constantly changing system that considers various factors to determine which content gets seen. LinkedIn keeps the specifics under wraps, which leads to a lot of misinformation and misconceptions about how to *"game"* the system.

The strategies I lay out in the *Laws of LinkedIn* aren't based on secret formulas or so-called insider knowledge. They come from real, hands-on experience—what's worked for me after years of posting, engaging, and building a following. These laws are rooted in tried-and-true methods that have helped me connect with my audience and grow my influence, not by manipulating an algorithm, but by consistently providing value through my content. The key is understanding that real success comes from delivering genuine, quality engagement—not trying to outsmart a system no one fully controls.

Am I ready to ship this to you?

I'll let you in on a little secret: I can't switch off. That's it, I admit it. I'm a workaholic, always moving, always creating, always striving to live an inspired life. So, when it came time to distil my mindset and process into a succinct book, it was quite the challenge to sit still. I usually can't.

What changed was attending an event with Jay Shetty at The Opera House. It was, in essence, a veiled promotion for his new book *The 8 Rules of Love*, but one question he asked struck a chord with me.

He had the entire audience stand and asked, *"In the last week, who here has been away from their phone for at least 7 hours? If you have, sit down."* About 10-15 people sat.

"In the last week, who here has been away from their phone for 5 hours?" Another 50-100 people sat…

As he continued to count down, more and more people in the hall sat down with each reduced hour. When he got to one hour, I was one of the few still standing. It hit me—what I'd been feeling for some time became real. I knew I needed to make changes if I was ever going to turn this book from *unmanifest* into *manifest*. Engaging less with technology lead to more meaningful time invested with family and worthy projects, like *The Laws of LinkedIn*.

I've poured my heart and soul into this book, capturing the very practices I use daily in the form of practical laws, stories, and personal anecdotes. It's my hope that this book will make a difference in the lives of millions of LinkedIn users for years to come.

How to read this book

This book has been structured much like a video game—by the way, I'm a bit of a retro gaming enthusiast. In the early chapters, you'll be introduced to the foundational laws, akin to learning the basic moves in a game. Think of these as the essential building blocks to understand, test, and master. As you progress through the later chapters, these blocks will start to work together, helping you unlock more advanced strategies and powerful techniques.

While each chapter can stand alone, you'll find that the concepts build upon one another. Reading from start to finish will allow you to absorb and apply the ideas more effectively. The laws outlined in this book serve as a roadmap to your LinkedIn success.

Inspired by Robert Greene's devious classic, *The 48 Laws of Power*, Greene discusses strategies for gaining power and influence, which parallels our approach in *The Laws of Linkedin*, so each chapter of this book includes:

- **Observing the Law**: Practical examples that illustrate the power of applying the law correctly.
- **Transgressing the Law**: Common pitfalls and cautionary tales of what happens when the law is ignored.
- **LinkedIn Judgment**: The rationale behind why the law works consistently in the context of LinkedIn.
- **Pro Tip**: Actionable advice or hacks you can immediately apply to your LinkedIn strategy.

Stick with me, dear reader, and you'll become a master builder of your LinkedIn craft. Just like in anything worth mastering, the more you put in, the more you'll get out.

Let's fire it up!
- CPH

A WARNING to the Reader

No one ever desired less recognition; everyone craves more. Some may cynically view these laws as the overenthusiastic musings of a salesman, redundant or irrelevant when applied to LinkedIn. But after nearly six years of intense use of the platform, I assure you, these laws are not only alive and relevant but also thriving.

Human psychology, driven by vanity and the need for significance, reveals predictable patterns—humans are predictable creatures. You can leverage these patterns to your advantage on LinkedIn. If you're tempted to dismiss this as a tongue-in-cheek guide or approach it with casual indifference, I encourage you to reflect on that choice.

These laws are for those truly committed to cultivating a genuine and loyal following. If that's what you're after, keep reading—and prepare yourself for significant success!!

Law #0 - Discover Your Tribe

> *Your tribe is waiting for you to show up.*
> — Marianne Williamson

Before diving into LinkedIn strategies, let's start with a fundamental question: Who is your ideal client (IC)? Imagine you're opening a restaurant. If I asked you what the most important part of any restaurant is, what would you say?

When I pose this question to my legal clients, colleagues, or during talks, responses often include *"Lighting," "Great steak," "Good music," "Fantastic chef,"* or *"Nice location."* Some even mention *"Ambience"* or *"Parking."* While these factors are important, the most crucial element for your restaurant (or any business) is a *"starving crowd."* If there's no demand for what you offer, nothing else matters. This is why we specialize in financing lawyers—because no one else is catering to them effectively. My joke is that nobody else wants to either!

<u>Observing the Law</u>

Consider the case of a friend who opened a donut shop in Darling Harbour Shopping Centre, a popular tourist spot in Sydney. Initially, everyone expected it to thrive due to the high foot traffic. However, a few weeks after opening, business began to decline. Despite having superior donuts, the shop was surrounded by other food vendors, leading to saturation and reduced customer interest. The paradox of choice also played a role—a confused mind tends to wander and go elsewhere.

Looks like the end, no? No, dear reader—the story does not end here.

My friend decided to close the Darling Harbour location and open a new shop in a less affluent but gentrified area of Sydney—Redfern. Initially, this seemed like a risky move. However, the result was remarkable: Business boomed as the shop became the go-to place for locals. With no other food options nearby, they had a monopoly on the market. The shop became a local sensation and thrived with booming business.

Transgressing the Law

In Australia, there are approximately 19,236 accredited mortgage brokers at the time of this writing, each capable of writing loans for a wide range of clients. When I ask these brokers who their ideal client is, the response is often, *"Everyone. I can serve anyone."*

This broad approach can be detrimental. According to a study published in the *Journal of Marketing Research,* businesses that adopt a generic target market often face challenges in developing effective marketing strategies. When you attempt to serve a larger audience, your messaging becomes diluted, leading to a lack of clarity about who you truly serve.

This phenomenon is evident in the mortgage industry. A colleague of mine, an experienced broker, once took pride in his ability to cater to a diverse clientele—from first-time homebuyers to seasoned property investors. Initially, he believed this would maximize his opportunities. However, as he spread his focus too thin, he found himself struggling to connect with clients on a deeper level. His marketing materials became a laundry list of services, failing to resonate with anyone in particular. Eventually, he discovered that his competition was better at capturing attention because they specialized, making it easier for them to convey their unique value.

The reality is that when your target audience is too broad, it's challenging to craft effective marketing messages that speak to specific pain points. Your tribe remains unclear, and your message gets lost in the noise of a crowded marketplace. A 2021 report from *McKinsey & Company* emphasizes that companies that focus on a well-defined target market can achieve up to 30% higher conversion rates compared to those with a generalized approach.

To avoid this pitfall, it's essential to narrow your focus. Identify the specific segments of clients who align best with your offerings. By homing in on a defined audience, you can tailor your marketing efforts, create compelling content, and build meaningful connections that will ultimately drive your success in the competitive landscape of LinkedIn and beyond.

Transgressing the Law: The Perils of Imitation

In the competitive landscape of legal finance, our company has worked diligently over the past seven years to carve out a niche in providing tailored home loans for lawyers. Recently, however, we discovered that another broking firm is attempting to mimic our approach and target our clients in the legal sector. Many of my contacts and referral partners in the legal field have brought this to my attention, and they remain steadfastly loyal.

This situation highlights a fundamental truth in business: while niching down can be a powerful strategy, being a copycat is never wise. Imitation may seem like a shortcut to success, but it often leads to a shallow understanding of the market and a lack of genuine connection with clients. Our brand recognition has been built on years of trust, expertise, and investment in relationships that cannot be replicated overnight. This competitor is not only facing an uphill battle to convince lawyers to switch to their services—but they are also missing the essence of what makes a brand truly valuable: authenticity.

As the saying goes, *"Good artists copy; great artists steal."* Yet, in the context of business, it's crucial to understand that true innovation and connection come from authenticity, not imitation. A competitor may attempt to imitate our strategies, but they will ultimately struggle to achieve the same level of trust and loyalty that we've cultivated.

As you navigate your own journey on LinkedIn, remember that it's not enough to simply follow trends or mimic what others are doing. Strive to be original, to express your unique voice, and to forge meaningful connections with your audience. Authenticity will set you apart in a crowded marketplace, allowing you to build a brand that stands the test of time. So, instead of copying others, focus on what makes you and your offerings distinct, and let that authenticity shine through in every interaction.

LinkedIn Judgement – Red Ocean & Blue Ocean

While there may be seven oceans in the world, in the realm of business, we often navigate just two: the red ocean and the blue ocean. This concept, popularized by W. Chan Kim and Renée Mauborgne in their book *Blue Ocean Strategy*, illustrates the competitive landscape of various markets.

The red ocean is characterized by fierce competition—akin to a bloody battlefield where every shark is vying for the same schools of fish. In a red ocean, businesses battle fiercely for limited market share, leading to price wars and diminished profits. According to a study published in the *Harvard Business Review*, companies operating in a red ocean often struggle with price wars, diminishing profits, and a battle for visibility.

This creates a landscape that is not only competitive but also exhausting for professionals trying to differentiate themselves.

Conversely, the blue ocean represents untapped market space, where the waters are calm, and opportunities abound. In this environment, fewer competitors exist, and the potential for innovation is vast. The concept encourages businesses to create new demand in an uncontested market space. For instance, *Cirque du Soleil* successfully transformed the entertainment industry by blending elements of circus and theatre, thereby creating a unique offering that attracted a diverse audience. Their innovative approach allowed them to thrive in a market that had previously been dominated by traditional circuses.

By aiming to swim in the blue ocean, you position yourself to stand out and thrive. Embrace the untapped potential of LinkedIn by identifying niche markets and unique value propositions that resonate with your target audience. Instead of competing for attention in a crowded space, focus on creating value that sets you apart. In this way, you can navigate the calm waters of opportunity and establish your unique presence in the LinkedIn ecosystem.

Pro Tip #1 – Create your Ideal Client Avatar

To find your tribe, follow this exercise to define your Ideal Client and nail that niche:

What is the benefit of my product?	
Who would it serve the most?	

Are they male, female, or gender-neutral?	
What age are they?	
What is their profession?	
Where do they spend their weekends?	
What do they do for fun?	
What are their hobbies?	
What are their major likes and dislikes?	
What keeps them up at night?	
What organisations are they a part of?	
What do they do for exercise?	
What social media platforms do they use?	
Is anyone else serving them like you?	
What makes you different from others for your tribe?	

The list is extensive, but not exhaustive, and should get you on your way to dial down and tap into your clients who desperately want what you're offering.

Pro Tip #2 – Call Out to Your Tribe

Once you've nailed your niche and identified your tribe, marketing becomes more focused. You'll understand their preferences, where they spend their time, and what keeps them up at night. This specificity reduces your advertising spend and enhances your targeting.

Research from the *Content Marketing Institute* shows that businesses that understand their audience's preferences and behaviours see 60% higher engagement rates compared to those that don't. Knowing your tribe allows you to craft messages that resonate deeply, creating a sense of connection and relevance. For instance, if your ideal client is a lawyer specializing in family law, sharing insights about work-life balance or showcasing success stories from other family law professionals can foster engagement and loyalty.

You may even want to start getting your morning coffee from the cafés they frequent, just a thought. Imagine walking into a local coffee shop that your clients love, striking up a conversation with the barista, and casually mentioning your work. Not only does this allow you to align yourself with their culture, but it also opens the door to authentic conversations. One lawyer I know frequented a local café popular with legal professionals. Over time, he built relationships with the staff and other patrons, which led to referrals and partnerships that significantly boosted his practice.

The current President of the Law Society of NSW, Brett McGrath, often holds meetings at La Riviera, the café next to the Law Society, where he can engage with everyone who walks in and enjoy serendipitous interactions. Smart move!

By immersing yourself in the spaces where your tribe gathers, you not only increase your visibility but also establish yourself as a trusted figure within the community. In the end, calling out to your tribe isn't just about marketing; it's about creating genuine connections that can lead to lasting relationships and business success.

Pro Tip #3 – Engage with Your Tribe's Content

Engagement is a two-way street. Don't just post content and hope for the best; actively engage with the content your tribe is sharing. Like, comment, and share their posts to build relationships and show that you're genuinely interested in what they have to say.

This not only helps you stay informed about their interests and pain points but also keeps you visible in their feed. Engaging with their content makes you more relatable and approachable, which can lead to meaningful connections and collaborations.

Think of it as a way to stay in tune with your tribe's heartbeat. Plus, it often leads to reciprocity, where they're more likely to engage with your content in return.

Remember, LinkedIn isn't just about broadcasting your message—it's about building a community. So, dive into the conversation and become a part of your tribe's daily online interactions!

Closing Thoughts: Dive Deep and Discover

So, dear reader, as you embark on this journey to discover your tribe, remember that finding your ideal clients is like fishing in the vast ocean of LinkedIn. The sea is full of potential connections, but not all schools of fish will suit your taste. Whether you're a shark or a minnow, the key is to find your niche and make waves in the blue ocean.

Imagine yourself as a master chef in that restaurant, serving up delectable dishes tailored to the unique palate of your clientele. The more you refine your menu to meet their desires, the more they'll flock to your establishment, making it the talk of the town. And as you engage with your tribe—understanding their likes, dislikes, and what keeps them awake at night—you'll not only become a familiar face but also a trusted resource.

So, grab your fishing rod (or, in our case, your laptop), cast your line into the depths of LinkedIn, and start exploring. Don't just wait for your ideal clients to swim by—create a splash that gets their attention. Nurture those connections and build relationships, because remember in this ocean, you're not just a business owner; you're a community builder.

As you venture forward, keep this in mind: your tribe is out there, waiting for someone who speaks their language, understands their needs, and delivers the value they crave. So, take the plunge, embrace the journey, and soon enough, you'll find yourself surrounded by the very people who will help you scale those seven-figure heights!

Now, go forth and discover your tribe—because they're just waiting for you to lead them to the treasures of LinkedIn!

Law #1 - Just Start

Just start. Start now. Fail often. Enjoy the ride.
— Seth Godin

Every time we create something new, we go from zero to one.
— Peter Thiel

When we launched Legal Home Loans in May of 2018, we were at a standing start. No one knew who we were. We had zero clients, zero marketing budget, and zero prospects. Or so we thought. I had a modest network at the time on LinkedIn of about 500 people, and I thought, *Why not try to tap into this?*.

So, I posted my first picture (see photo below). It was me signing my LHL contract with Andrew, my business partner. My God, it felt good. For a few reasons, it was my first major post in my new role, second, it was personal (not just about business – and business is personal), third, I'd started. *"You drop a pebble in a pond; you get ripples. Soon the ripples are across the whole pond"* – Bruce Lee, *Dragon: The Bruce Lee Story*

THE LAWS OF LINKEDIN

*My business partner, Andrew Johnson, and I
signing my LHL contract in May 2018.*

I had a quote above the photo, a brief note, and then the photo. To my surprise, it became our highest-performing post. This success motivated me to connect with more people, led to a surge in new connections and venture into the next level of content creation: Video.

At the time, LinkedIn was not known for video when we launched Legal Home Loans. Naturally, we thought it would be a cracking place to start. We created a series called *Whiteboard Wednesdays*. We didn't realise that posting a heretical 7-minute video is sacrilege when it comes to the bite size world of content, but we did it anyway. You also have to remember, not many people were doing video at all at the time on LinkedIn. You can see our debut episode here:

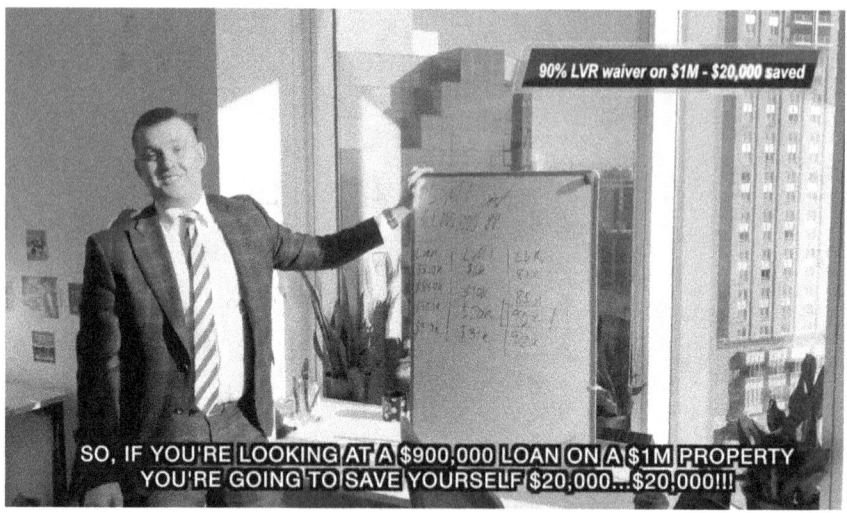

*Whiteboard Wednesdays Ep.1 – LVR & LMI with Andrew Johnson
Source: YouTube – Cullen P. Haynes – Circulate to Percolate
https://www.youtube.com/watch?v=PNKOztnGZJA&t=57s*

In this debut episode, you'll notice the video is bright and energetic, featuring Andrew (AJ), my business partner, holding the whiteboard. There are Grant Cardone posters in the background, and the overall quality isn't perfect. But you know what? We had started. And we knew it would standout because no one else was doing it; let alone editing. I used Final Cut Pro to edit it, marking the beginning of our journey to building a significant following on LinkedIn.

Pro Tip #1 – Your Persuasion Stack

Let me be honest: I'm not the best broker or the most prestigious person in finance. I'm neither the oldest nor the most renowned. But here's the truth—no other broker brings my unique life experience to the table. No other person in the industry has been a professional magician with the sleight of hand, mind, and storytelling abilities to pull it off. No other broker needed the polished customer service to have dinner with John Cleese as a hotel manager or looked after Seal or faced the wrath of Jon Bon Jovi (long story!). No one else in the industry has had to X-ray patients who are dying from cancer and possesses the care and empathy instilled from that experience. No other person in my industry has my technological savvy that that I honed over many years while cutting videos for hotels and during my time at Macquarie bank and now, because of all that, my persuasion stack makes me exceptionally effective at what I do.

There are things about you that no one else knows. Your experiences and skills are unique, much like a fingerprint. Your authentic persuasion stack, which you bring to your business and LinkedIn presence, is something to be valued and cherished.

Tap into it!

Observing the Law

There's a video circulating the internet. It's of Peter Dinklage, the actor famous for his role as Tyrian Lannister in the massive hit *Game of Thrones*. In it, he reflects on his soul-crushing job as a data enterer at *Professional Examination Services*. He admits, *"I hated that job, and I clung to that job."* Yet, Dinklage had the courage to pursue acting—a risk that paid off. We may never have heard of him if he hadn't pursued his passion. There's always the risk you'll fail. His story exemplifies Samuel Beckett's immortal words which Dinklage also shares:

> *"Ever tried. Ever failed. No Matter. Try Again. Fail again. Fail Better."*

https://www.youtube.com/watch?v=eCBnbRmXQtU
Source – Motivation Hub.

Our first video series quickly evolved. We began with daily posts, then moved to two a day, and soon we were posting seven times daily—more than any other broker at the time. This growth led to additional video series like *Vehicle Victory, Car Wash Conversations, Your Money – Your Way, The LHL Stories Series,* and now to the *Live with Cullen Haynes* stream and podcast. We have launched 11 different series and counting, and we wouldn't have ever done it if we hadn't taken the initial leap.

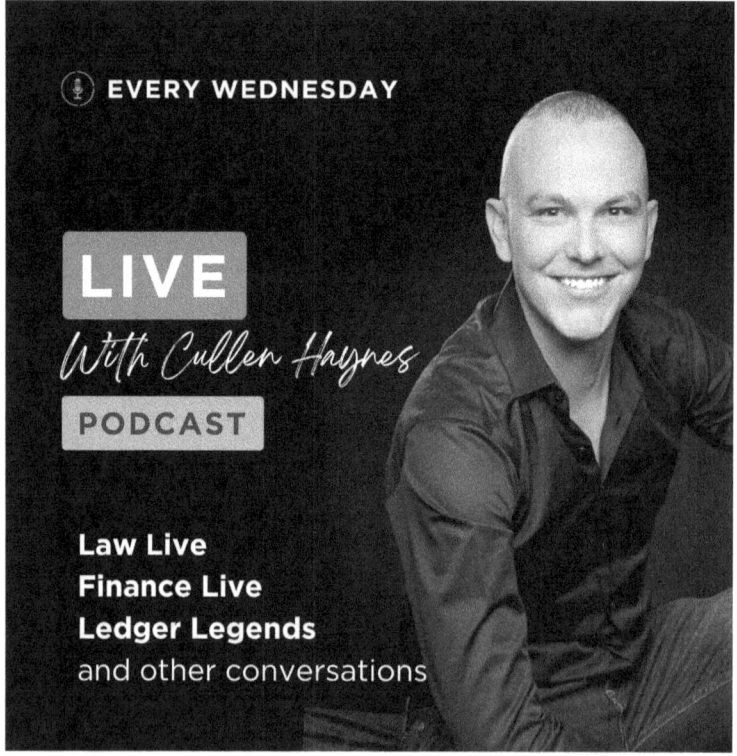

Live with Cullen Haynes podcast series
Subscribe here: https://podcasts.apple.com/au/podcast/live-with-cullen-haynes/id1639782288

Closing Thoughts: The Power of Initiation

As I look back on our journey since launching Legal Home Loans, I can't help but reflect on the profound impact of those initial steps. We started with more than just a dream, a willingness to embrace the unknown, and a belief that our unique experiences could carve a niche in a crowded marketplace. Remember, the first step is often the hardest, but it's also the most transformative.

Seth Godin's call to *"just start"* resonates deeply in today's fast-paced world, where perfectionism often paralyses potential. Each post, each video, and each connection we made along the way was a testament to the power of initiation. When we dared to share our story, we not only sparked interest but also ignited conversations that would shape our brand and our lives.

Think of Peter Dinklage's journey from data entry to the glitz of Hollywood. He could have remained stagnant, clinging to the security of that uninspiring job. Instead, he took the leap, embracing the uncertainty that comes with pursuing passion. Like Dinklage, you too have the capacity to transform your circumstances by simply starting. Embrace the fear of failure; it's the bedrock of growth.

Our path evolved from timid posts to bold content creation, ultimately leading to the launch of eleven distinct video series. Each series was a stepping stone, a result of that pivotal decision to start. By taking action, we discovered our voice, our audience, and our impact.

So, I challenge you to let go of hesitation and embrace action. Whether you're sharing insights, exploring new ideas, or simply connecting with like-minded individuals, every action propels you closer to your goals. The road may be uncertain, but remember: every master was once an apprentice, and every great achievement begins with a single courageous step.

Now, go forth and make your mark on LinkedIn. It starts with just one step, and you never know where it may lead. Every great achievement begins with the courage to start. Every great master was once an apprentice. The path to success is paved with those first brave steps. Prepare yourself, for our next law awaits—a deeper dive into harnessing the power of your newfound momentum. Let's keep moving forward together!

Law #2 - There's No Limit: Post Now, Post Often

Content is fire; social media is gasoline.
— Jay Baer

Dear reader, please don't trust the self-anointed *"experts"* who suggest that you can only post once or twice a week. As Grant Cardone puts it, *"Posting online is like kicking bricks in the ocean."* You can't max out or over post as long as you're delivering quality content consistently. So, go all out!

Uncle G and Me – "Be Obsessed or Be Average"

Start with a routine and build up!

At the height of our business growth phase, I was posting 7-10 times a day on LinkedIn. This may seem excessive to some. However, for my tribe of 90,000 lawyers in Australia—it didn't even make a dent. More posts mean more visibility. You might see less engagement per post due to dilution, but that's expected. So, let's dive into how consistency can lead to effective posting.

Here was my daily posting schedule back then:

- 2-3 Videos
- 2-3 Photos
- 1 Text-Only Post
- 1 CTA (Call to Action)

As our brand grew and family demands increased, I shifted to a more manageable rhythm of 4-5 posts a day:

- 1 Running post, book review or Quote
- 1 Poll (Yes/No)
- 1 #LegendOfLaw post
- 1 Video Snippet from Live with Cullen Haynes
- 1 Finance Post (Educational or CTA)

My tribe knows me for my positivity and enthusiasm, it's something many note when they connect with me, so my content is always upbeat and sunny. Be true to who you are.

Observing the Law

Build up your posting gradually. To facilitate this, consider the following routine:

- **Week 1**: Start with a text-only post once a day. Just text. Share an anonymous client conversation or a daily anecdote.

- **Week 2**: Increase to 2 posts per day and include a photo with a client or supplier.
    - *Jump to* **[Law #20 – Circulate to Percolate – Elevate Others Above Yourself]**
- **Week 3**: Post a 60-second video of yourself.
    - *Jump to* **[Law #17 – Video Killed the Article Star]**
- **Week 4**: Introduce polls and test different yes/no dynamics.
    - *Jump to* **[Law #19 - Polls of Persuasion: The Yes/No Paradigm]**

So, there you have it, you thought you had nothing to post about. Soon, you'll find you have more content ideas than time to post them.

A great example of someone who follows a structured posting schedule is Edward Zia, LinkedIn Certified Consultant and Influencer. His schedule looks something like this:

- 1-2 posts – Video of him out and about
- 1-2 posts – Awesome winners' post
- 1-2 posts – Photos of him with food
- 1 post – CTA post
- 1 post – Poll, usually, *"Do you love LinkedIn?"*

Transgressing the Law

Posting only clickbait or low-value sales pitches will result in weak engagement and subpar leads and meetings booked with your clients as opposed to adding value through quality consistent consent.

There was one banker, turned LinkedIn coach, who charged a hefty monthly fee to his clients. His advice? Post *"1-2 times a week max."*

Very soon, his clients grew frustrated with the poor returns. Where is that coach now? Back working at the bank.

I also once knew a broker colleague who decided to jump on the LinkedIn bandwagon. He was eager to get results quickly and started posting flashy headlines like *"The Lowest Rates in the Market"* or *"The Banks with the Best Offers"* He was convinced that sensationalism would bring in leads.

For a while, it seemed like his approach worked—he got lots of likes and comments. But when it came to actual business, the leads were cold, and the conversations were shallow. His posts weren't providing real value or insight, just empty promises.

Eventually, his business plateaued, and he realized that his strategy wasn't sustainable. He pivoted to sharing genuine advice and valuable insights about the real estate market. His engagement skyrocketed, and he started seeing meaningful interactions and high-quality leads.

The lesson? People are not looking for flashy gimmicks; they want authentic, valuable content. Without it, you're just shouting into the void.

Pro Tip #1 – Genius Ideas

If you're like me and your mind races with ideas, have a system to capture them, especially those that come to you unexpectedly; like those in the shower. Notes on your phone is a great way stockpile your nuggets. So is texting yourself. What I find most helpful is sending emails to myself during the day of great content ideas, so I don't forget.

Never trust your memory. Many times, I've had a zinger of a content idea that I neglected to store. Very soon I've forgotten it. Recently, I've been using Monday.com which has a great task and tick list which is very sleek and easy to use. I also do this for my business, sales meetings, calls to make and other tasks.

Pro Tip #2 – We are Legion

Maintain consistent formatting across your posts. *Jump to [Law #3 Repetition & Consistency are Key ✎]* for more on this.

Embrace the boundless potential of your voice. Post now, post often, and let your message ripple through the LinkedIn feed waves. Remember, there's no ROI on playing small – only by seizing every opportunity and sharing bolding can you unlock the true power of your presence. The more you post authentically and truthfully, the more connections you'll make, enhancing your overall impact.

Closing Thoughts: Unleash Your Voice

As you step into the vibrant world of LinkedIn, remember that the only limits that exist are the ones you place on yourself. Whether you start with one post a day or dive headfirst into multiple daily updates, the key is consistency and authenticity. Embrace the chaos of your thoughts, capture those fleeting ideas, and let your unique voice be heard.

As Walt Disney wisely said, *"I resent the limitations on my own imagination."* Don't allow anyone else to box you in—least of all self-proclaimed *"experts."* Instead, use your creativity to build a community that thrives on your insights and experiences. Your tribe is waiting, and each post is an opportunity to connect, educate, and inspire.

Picture this: the moment you hit that *"post"* button, you're not just sharing content; you're planting seeds in the minds of your audience. Who knows what could grow from those little seeds—relationships, opportunities, and collaborations that can transform your professional journey.

So go ahead—post often, post fearlessly. The world needs to hear your voice, your story, and your expertise. You have a tribe waiting to be inspired, and you hold the key to unlocking the connections that will elevate your career. Embrace the endless possibilities and let your LinkedIn presence shine!

Now, take a deep breath and dive in. Your journey begins with that first post—make it count!

Law #3 - LinkedIn is Not a Resume: See & Be Seen

Who you are speaks so loudly, I can't hear what you're saying.
— *Ralph Waldo Emerson*

A common misconception is that LinkedIn serves only as a virtual CV or online resume. While it can function as such, it has the potential to be so much more.

You can either be a solo practitioner staying small or elevate your game to impact hundreds or even thousands. As my friend Dr. John McGill says, *"If you give a child a hammer and they don't know how to use it, it becomes just another toy."* The same applies to LinkedIn. If you don't understand how to use it effectively, it too will become just another toy, and like many social media platforms, it will end up using you rather than the other way around.

As the old adage goes, *"You get out what you put in."* LinkedIn can be more than a mere record; it can be a source of great inspiration.

Ignore those who use LinkedIn solely as a resume or criticize your 10X efforts. I guarantee that such critics often have no profile picture, minimal posts, and fewer than 500 connections. They're more likely to be inactive or engage in trolling. Set the example yourself. Engagement, whether positive or negative, has value.

"Here are strategies to enhance your LinkedIn profile for maximum impact and weapons grade persuasion level.

Front and Centre – The Ideal Profile Pic

You're never fully dressed without a smile. A smile is an essential element of your professional image.

Dress your best and ensure it's in line with your brand, whatever that means for you.

It doesn't have to be a suit and tie (that's my brand for my clientele), but it should feature you smiling and exuding energy in a clear, crisp, zoomed-in, front-on shot.

Observing the Law

Profiles to check and follow for inspiration:

- Alistair Marshall - https://www.linkedin.com/in/alistairmarshall1967/?originalSubdomain=au
- Bill Ash - https://www.linkedin.com/in/bill-ash-494a5145/
- David Gale - https://www.linkedin.com/in/david-gale-6404b5a7/
- Edward Zia – https://www.linkedin.com/in/edwardzia/
- Hayder Shkara - https://www.linkedin.com/in/haydershkara/
- James d'Apice - https://www.linkedin.com/in/jamesdapice/
- Lara Wentworth - https://www.linkedin.com/in/lara-wentworth/
- Pepe Kish - https://www.linkedin.com/in/perpetua-kish-914887117/
- Peter Hunt - https://www.linkedin.com/in/bill-ash-494a5145/
- Reena Strehle - https://www.linkedin.com/in/reenastrehle/
- Stefanie Costi - https://www.linkedin.com/in/stefanie-costi/

Transgressing the Law

Photos that are blurry, taken at a party, screenshot from zoom, little to no clothes on or dressed in pyjamas. Here's some of my more light-hearted anecdotes to illustrate the pitfalls of using low-quality LinkedIn photos

1. **The *"Pixelated Pioneer"*:** Imagine a LinkedIn profile photo that's so pixelated, it looks like it was taken with a 1990s digital camera. I once had a connection who used a photo so blurry that I mistook it for an abstract piece of art. When they showed up to a networking event, I almost didn't recognize them because their photo didn't do them justice. Lesson learned: if your profile pic looks like a Rorschach test, it might be *time for an upgrade!*
2. **The *"Party Crasher"*:** Another connection of mine once used a LinkedIn photo from a wild office party where they were mid-cheer with a drink in hand. The photo made them look like the life of the party, but it didn't exactly scream professionalism. When I finally met them in person, I had to do a double take. They were nothing like *the party animal in their photo. Moral of the story: LinkedIn isn't the place for your "I'm having a great time"* party pics.
3. **The *"Zoom Screenshot Saga"*:** I once connected with someone whose LinkedIn profile photo was a screenshot from a Zoom call. You know, the one with their camera turned off, showing just a blank black screen with their name. When they added a new photo, it was from a Zoom call where their camera was on, but they had their dog in their lap. It's great to be casual, but for LinkedIn, let's leave the pets out of the professional image;

unless that's your business or you want people to know you love dogs!

4. **The *"Pyjama Professional"*:** There's always that one profile photo where the person is clearly in their pyjamas, maybe with a bedhead look, holding a cup of coffee. It's like they were in the middle of a Sunday morning and thought, *"Hey, why not update my LinkedIn profile while I'm at it?"* While we all love a comfy weekend, it's worth saving the PJs for weekend selfies, not professional profiles.

5. **The *"Blurry Mystery"*:** A friend of mine once had a LinkedIn photo so blurry that it looked like they were trying to be incognito. I'm sure from time to time when someone tried to connect with them, they had to ask, *"Is that you in the photo, or am I trying to connect with a shadow?"* The lesson here: if your profile pic needs a detective to identify you, it's time for a clearer shot!

I think you get the picture, pun intended. The importance of a clear image cannot be overstated.

However, it's better to have some photo, rather than not at all, otherwise you look like a bot.

It's important to note that, most trolls will have either a poor-quality photo or none at all.

Background Photos

From my experience, the LinkedIn algorithm – and more importantly, the people who follow you, love seeing group shots. Why? Group photos are valuable as they signal your influence and collaboration with others in your field. A well-composed group photo tells your audience that you're not just out there on your own; you have the magnetism and leadership to amass a following. You have unique persuasion stack. So, if you run a business or work within a company or family office, get a photo with your team. If you're an author, showcase a shot of you holding your book. And if you're a marketer or consultant, get a picture with your tribe at an event or function. It's about showing you're in the mix and involved in your professional community, not just on the sidelines. Remember, on LinkedIn, it's not about selling the steak, but selling the sizzle – people want to see the energy and connection you bring! I've always loved that analogy, even as a vegetarian.

My current background shot of my team at our conference in Fiji – Feb 2024

Grab Attention with Your Profile Headline

Imagine you're at a crowded networking event, where hundreds of lawyers are mingling, each one armed with their own elevator pitch. With over 1 Billion users on LinkedIn, think of your profile as your personal billboard in this bustling metropolis. Your headline is your best chance to shine and say, *"Hey, look at me!"*

An impactful headline, paired with a well-written, personalized About section, can transform your profile from just another face in the crowd to a must-meet connection.

When crafting your headline, ask yourself: What do you want a first-time visitor to know about you? How can you help them? What's your secret sauce? Remember, your profile isn't just about you; it's about your audience too.

Take my headline as an example: "🏆 Award-Winning Finance Broker for Lawyers ⚖️ Time-Pressed Barristers 👦⚖️ Top-Tier Partners 👧💼 CA's, Actuaries & Analysts 📋 MPA Top 100 Broker Firm 💯 MBA 🎓 Distance Runner 🏃‍♂️ Book Fanatic 📚 7 Days 0499 913 930 📱." It's like a quick snack that's both satisfying and filling—it showcases my unique qualifications while inviting engagement.

Make Headlines:

- **Be Concise**: Aim for clarity while keeping your headline brief. The ideal length is about 120 characters—enough to encapsulate your brand without overwhelming the reader.
- **Use Emojis Wisely**: Emojis can add a visual element to your headline, making it more engaging and approachable.

However, use them sparingly and appropriately to maintain professionalism.
- **Tailor to Your Audience**: Consider who you want to attract. Are you seeking clients, partners, or job opportunities? Tailor your language and focus to align with their interests and needs.

An attention-grabbing profile headline is essential for standing out on LinkedIn. Think of your headline as a warm handshake—it's the first impression that can open the door to connections and opportunities. So, get out there and make your headline unforgettable!

Observing the Law

In the vast sea of LinkedIn profiles, the visuals we choose represent our professional identity and can speak volumes about our professional identity. Research from 3M Corporation and Zogby International. (2001). *The Visual Communication Revolution.* indicates that **visual content** is processed **60,000 times faster** than text, which means that the right images can significantly enhance your profile's first impression. A compelling background photo not only adds visual interest but also communicates the essence of your brand or team.

According to a study by **LinkedIn itself *LinkedIn. (2019):The Ultimate Guide to LinkedIn for Business,*** profiles with a background image receive **up to 14 times more profile views** than those without one. This is crucial in a professional landscape where differentiation can lead to new opportunities. A well-chosen background photo serves as a conversation starter, providing context and intrigue that invites viewers to learn more about you.

Effective Uses of Background Photos

Many successful professionals leverage this tool to highlight their expertise, values, or even their team dynamics. For instance, a law firm may choose a background that showcases its team in action, while a motivational speaker might use an inspiring landscape that aligns with their message.

Here are some profiles that exemplify the power of effective background imagery:

- **Alistair Marshall**: Alistair's background highlights his new book, visually representing his commitment to sharing knowledge and expertise. This choice not only promotes his work but also positions him as a thought leader in his field. Explore his profile here - https://www.linkedin.com/in/alistairmarshall1967/?originalSubdomain=au
- **Clarissa Rayward**: Clarissa's background is tailored to her branding, incorporating elements that highlight her expertise in family law. Her visuals communicate warmth and professionalism, inviting connections. Explore her profile here - https://www.linkedin.com/in/clarissarayward/
- **Dom Nesci**: Dom's background features a vibrant image of his team, emphasizing collaboration and connection. This visual reinforces his brand as a leader who values teamwork and community. Check out his profile here - https://www.linkedin.com/in/domnesci/
- **Jerome Doraisamy**: Jerome's background captures a moment from an awards night where he is hosting for the *Lawyers Weekly*, showcasing his involvement in the industry and his

commitment to celebrating achievements. This image conveys both professionalism and charisma, inviting viewers to connect with him on a deeper level. Visit his profile here - https://www.linkedin.com/in/jeromedoraisamy/
- **Lucy Dickens**: Lucy uses a professional and visually appealing background that resonates with her brand identity. It enhances her image as a credible and approachable leader in her field. Check out her profile here - https://www.linkedin.com/in/lucy-dickens/
- **Pepe Kish**: Pepe's background showcases her dedication to family dispute resolution, reflecting her professional ethos and making her profile relatable to potential clients. You can view her profile here - https://www.linkedin.com/in/perpetua-kish-914887117/
- **Mario Bekes**: Mario's background image emphasizes his expertise in human intelligence, providing insight into his professional focus and inviting viewers to connect over shared interests. Check out his profile here - https://www.linkedin.com/in/mariobekes-human-intelligence-expert/
- **Marnie Cooper**: Marnie's background reflects her commitment to family dispute resolution, reinforcing her message and attracting the right audience to her profile. Visit her profile here - https://www.linkedin.com/in/marniecooperfamilydisputeresolutionmediator/

Select background images that align with your professional identity and you can enhance your visibility and engage your audience more effectively. Remember, your LinkedIn profile is often the first impression potential clients or collaborators will have of you—make it count with visuals that tell your story.

Transgressing the Law

Using stock images from Google, generic advertisements, or bland, uninspiring colours. You've likely seen it for yourself. A Director at Macquarie, whom I worked with, took personal branding so seriously that he outright banned any use of Google for photos. He said, *"A random stock image will never tell me anything worthwhile about you..."* Timeless wisdom indeed, and he was absolutely right. If your visuals don't reflect or align your unique voice or story, they're just noise in a crowded space.

History is replete with companies that transgressed this law, especially when the service didn't match up with their uninspiring brand or marketing campaign: -

- **Woolworths *"Fresh Food People"* Campaign (2010s)**
    - If you're from Australia, you'll be all too familiar with this one. For years, Woolies positioned itself as "The Fresh Food People" aiming to emphasize its commitment to high-quality produce. However, many customers called the actual freshness and quality into question. This disconnect between the brand's messaging and the actual client experience led to a perceived lack of authenticity and criticism. Woolies now focuses on the stories behind the farmers and suppliers in their ads and within their stores which I think is a wise move.
- **Australia Post's *"Sending Love"* Campaign**
    - Aus Post had the best intentions behind a campaign aimed to evoke an emotional connection with its "Sending Love" theme. Despite the emotional intent, customers

faced significant delays. A discrepancy underscoring the importance of branding efforts that are inspiring and match what is actually being delivered. Playing devil's advocate, if they'd focussed on the people that make these messages of love possible, despite the delays that may come up, customers may have found it more endearing and been able to forgive service lapses.

#Yes – Selecting Your Hashtags

LinkedIn's algorithm lets you select five hashtags that define your content, showcasing your core focus—essentially defining what you're all about. For me, my five hashtags that capture my unique energy are:

- **#Lawyers**
- **#Motivation**
- **#Inspiration**
- **#Investing**
- **#Books**

Research shows that relevant hashtags significantly enhance your visibility and engagement on the platform. According to a study by *Buffer,* posts that include at least one hashtag can see an increase in engagement of up to **12.6%** compared to those without. This is particularly relevant on LinkedIn, where users are increasingly using hashtags to discover content that resonates with their interests.

For example, the **#Lawyers** hashtag has over **1.1 million followers** on LinkedIn, which means that when I use it, my content has the potential to reach a vast audience of legal professionals and enthusiasts. Similarly, hashtags like **#Motivation** and **#Inspiration** attract individuals looking for uplifting content, further broadening my reach.

Running is another passion of mine, something I've been doing since primary school. If a sixth tag becomes available, I'd definitely add "Running." The **#Running** community on LinkedIn is also robust, with a diverse range of professionals sharing their fitness journeys, networking, and supporting each other.

Now, think about the five things that define you. If people were asked to describe you and your business, what would they say? Take a moment to think: What five hashtags define you? And which ones have a large enough following to amplify your reach?

Research by *HubSpot* indicates that hashtags with a larger following can amplify your reach considerably. For instance, hashtags like **#Investing** and **#Books** have followers in the hundreds of thousands, making them effective tools for increasing your visibility. Conversely, if your hashtag is too niche, like **#AtlanticScubadiving**, chances are you won't attract many followers or engagement.

Each of my categories has followers ranging from **100,000** to millions. These are distinct from your content hashtags, which can help dial down your audience as needed per post. By strategically selecting hashtags that resonate with your brand and have a broad following, you can significantly enhance your presence on LinkedIn and connect with your ideal audience.

Observing the Law

Hashtags hold real power, as social media algorithms rely on them to tag and discover content that represents you. According to *Sprout Social*, posts with at least one hashtag can increase engagement by **12.6%** on average. For LinkedIn, which prioritizes content discovery through hashtags, choosing the right ones can be a game changer for your visibility and connection with your target audience.

The key is to be as specific as possible while aligning yourself with hashtags that have enough reach. General hashtags might give you a broad audience, but niche hashtags can help you connect deeply with your ideal clients. The key is balancing popular hashtags with niche ones that reflect your unique brand.

For example, a study by *Hootsuite* found that posts that include three to five hashtags perform better than those with fewer or more. This means that selecting hashtags like **#Lawyers** and **#Investing** can place your content in front of a focused audience while still taking advantage of a larger community.

People to Follow for Great #Examples:
- **James d'Apice**: Known for his insights into legal matters and how they intersect with social media, James effectively utilizes hashtags to reach fellow legal professionals. Check out Jame d'Apice on LinkedIn here: https://www.linkedin.com/in/jamesdapice/
- **Peter Hunt** - As a Partner at McCabes Lawyers and the author behind *The Arched Eyebrow Review*, Peter blends legal expertise with a passion for theatre. His insightful blog provides

detailed play reviews, and his engaging profile—featuring event photos—showcases his expertise in both law and public speaking. Follow his journey here: https://www.linkedin.com/in/peter-hunt-7b18023/?originalSubdomain=au
- **Reena Strehle**: A thought leader in diversity and inclusion, Reena uses hashtags like **#Diversity** and **#Inclusion** to not only promote her message but to engage with a community passionate about change. You can find her herehttps://www.linkedin.com/in/reenastrehle/
- **Stefani Costi**: With her focus on mental health and well-being in the legal profession, Stefani's strategic use of hashtags like **#MentalHealth** connects her with lawyers seeking support and resources. Follow her journey here - https://www.linkedin.com/in/stefanie-costi/

By observing how these influencers effectively use hashtags, you can glean strategies that resonate with your audience. For instance, they focus on building a narrative around their posts while aligning with hashtags that amplify their message.

So, take a page from their playbooks and use hashtags as a powerful tool to enhance your presence on LinkedIn. Remember, the right hashtags can transform your posts from merely visible to truly impactful.

Pro Tip #1 – Gone in 60 Seconds: Profile Video

This feature may have been removed by the time you're reading this, but a 60-second video on your profile is a powerful way to showcase your brand. A dynamic or iconic background, like Sydney Harbour Bridge, can highlight who you are, what you're about, where you're located, who you serve, the content you post, and why people should follow you.

When people land on your profile, they'll not only see your photo but also your video, creating an instant connection; *instant rapport* as Jim Rohn would coin it. This is a powerful persuasion technique. I've lost count of how many times I've been stopped in Sydney's CBD and complimented on my content. I don't say this to impress you, but to impress upon you the importance of making your profile shine!

In the LinkedIn landscape, being seen is just as vital as seeing others. Think of LinkedIn not as a static, stilted resume, but as a dynamic stage where engagement and visibility create lasting impressions. Show up, engage actively and with insights and let your presence resonate. After all, the more you put yourself out there, the more opportunities you'll attract. Be visible, be engaged, and watch your network – and your influence – grow!

Pro Tip #2: Why Getting Verified on LinkedIn is a Game Changer

Imagine standing in a crowd of thousands—everyone vying for attention, pushing their personal brand or business. Now picture yourself with a verified badge, instantly recognizable. It's a signal that says, *I'm credible. I'm trusted.* Getting Verified on LinkedIn isn't just about a shiny blue tick—it's a powerful credibility boost that increases trust, reach, and engagement.

Here's why it matters: Studies show that verified accounts on social platforms see a significant uptick in engagement. On LinkedIn specifically, verified accounts report up to a **20-25% increase in profile**

views. Why? Validated profiles build trust. A *LinkedIn study* revealed that profiles with verified credentials are 30% more likely to receive connection requests and messages from prospects. More connections, more visibility, more influence.

So how do you get Verified? LinkedIn's verification process ensures that you are who you say you are. Here's how to make it happen:

1. **Build a strong profile**: Make sure your profile is polished—this includes a professional photo, complete work history, and consistent messaging across your headline and summary.
2. **Apply for LinkedIn verification**: Under your settings, find the 'Verify Your Identity' option, and follow the steps. You'll likely need to provide a government-issued ID and proof of employment or business registration.
3. **Engage regularly**: The LinkedIn algorithm rewards active and verified users. Once you're verified, show LinkedIn you're serious—post consistently, engage with your network, and share high-value content that reflects your expertise.

Getting Verified is like unlocking a hidden LinkedIn feature that skyrockets your influence. It's one of those *small but mighty* moves that can open doors you didn't even know were there. Don't miss out on the opportunity to be seen and trusted in a crowded digital space.

Closing Thoughts: Show Up, Stand Out

As we wrap up Law #3, remember this: LinkedIn is not just a digital resume; it's a dynamic platform for connection, influence, and impact. It's about harnessing the power of visibility and crafting your professional narrative in a way that resonates with others. As Ralph Waldo Emerson reminds us, *"Who you are speaks so loudly, I can't hear what you're saying."* This rings especially true on LinkedIn.

By viewing your profile through the lens of a vibrant community rather than a static document, you can elevate your presence. Engage, share, and connect. Invest time in curating your profile images, showcasing your unique voice, and actively participating in conversations that matter to you. The critics who dismiss LinkedIn as merely a resume? Let them. They're often the same folks hiding behind low-quality photos and minimal engagement, missing out on the vast potential this platform offers.

Use your profile to shine a spotlight on your values and expertise. Think of it as your own personal stage—who do you want to be seen as? What story do you want to tell? Don't be afraid to step into the spotlight. Show your energy, your passion, and your expertise. As we've seen with the profiles that inspire us, it's not just about the achievements on paper; it's about the connections you make and the lives you touch.

So, as you venture forth into this landscape, armed with the knowledge of how to use LinkedIn to its fullest potential, remember this: LinkedIn is an opportunity to be seen—not just as a professional, but as a person with a unique story to tell. Be bold, be engaging, and be you. **Embrace the art of visibility.**

Now, go out there, put your best foot forward, and remember that every interaction on LinkedIn can open doors to new opportunities. Your journey is just beginning, and the world is waiting to see what you can achieve. Let's turn that 'resume' into a vibrant career canvas and remember: **See and be seen!**

Call to Action

Ready to take your LinkedIn presence to the next level? Start by revamping your profile picture and background image today. Share your journey, engage with others, and watch as new opportunities unfold. If you're looking for more tips, strategies, or inspiration, don't hesitate to reach out—let's connect and elevate our LinkedIn game together!

Law #4 - Repetition & Consistency are Key 🔑

> Small disciplines repeated with consistency everyday
> lead to great achievements gained slowly over time.
> — John C Maxwell

Now. What content should you post? We'll dive into more ideas for the 'what' in a later Law. For now, let's focus on the question *"How should I get started?"* The key is to make it sustainable—something you can go back to again and again making it easy for yourself.

Your content should align with what your tribe values most from you.

Because I'm passionate about self-enrichment, quotes became my method for showing my tribe what I stood for when I began. Since 2018, I've posted a quote every single day. Here's the template I started and still use:

> 💎 *"Whether you think you can or think you can't, you're right"*
> Henry Ford

Hit Follow 🏀 Like. Share. Comment. 🙏 Make It Count 😊

#Lawyers #Motivation #Inspiration #Leadership #Books

The sign-off, starting from *"Hit Follow"* is my post's catchphrase. I use it in all my posts. More on that later.

The Benefits of Consistency

Here's why this method works:

1) **Simplifies the process** – By using a template (whether it's a quote, video or post), you reduce the bulk of the work. You only need to change the main body or front portion each day.
2) **Builds audience expectation** - Your followers will get used to your posting style, content and frequency, making them more likely to engage. James d'Apice and I exemplify this principle—we regularly stop by each other's posts.
3) **Provides structure** – A set structure helps ensure consistency. You know that every day you can post a quote, video, poll, or other content type without starting from scratch.
4) **Enables testing and iteration** – With a routine, you can test what works and tweak what doesn't, then rinse and repeat.

Observing the Law

Here's my daily routine. I stick to a similar layout every day (except on holidays when I might scale back or adjust the content):

1) Quote
2) Post on running or a book I'm reading
3) Video snippet from a Live with Cullen Haynes
4) Finance post, elevation through education (non-salesy)
5) Poll (kept positive, question framed negatively – More on this later)
6) *Meanwhile on Call with Cullen* (CTA a call-to-action post)

Each post follows a similar patter & pattern, ensuring consistency in both format and frequency. If daily posting feels overwhelming, you can spread this content over a week to start small.

Pro Tip 1 – Open to Everything, Attached to Nothing

As my late, great mentor, Wayne Dyer, aptly put, *"The key to a successful life is to keep your mind open to everything and attached to nothing."* I'm not suggesting you stick to the same routine indefinitely. After all, the definition of madness is repeating the same action and expecting different results.

What I'm advocating is structuring your content to ensure it gets posted and engaged with. As Jim Rohn wisely said, *"The unread book won't help you."* Similarly, the unposted post won't help you either.

The goal is to make your life easier – and make you more likely to follow through. The harder a task is, the less likely you are to do it. As James Clear explains in Atomic Habits, you need to make it obvious and be deliberate. A rubric and schedule are fantastic ways to do that.

Transgressing the Law

Anyone who knows me knows that my pet peeve is **clickbait**—content designed solely for quick engagement. Overusing irrelevant memes, gifs, or vapid content—like viral TikTok trends or the latest "kid and the coke can" video—might get more views in the short term, but it comes at a cost. It's content for content's sake. You've probably encountered influencers who do this, sacrificing authenticity for quick engagement. Think about viral videos like the **"Chewbacca Mom."** Sure, it attracted millions of views, but beyond a laugh, what value did it provide? When you consistently share content like this, it's **content for content's sake**, and your audience knows it.

Take **David 'Avocado' Wolfe** as an example. While he's an engaging advocate for the vegan lifestyle, his Instagram feed is flooded with this kind of redundant content. Despite his strong message, it often gets lost among the memes and unrelated posts. His story illustrates a critical point: **unoriginality is noticeable.** Your followers have likely seen it all before, and each recycled meme or clickbait post subtly erodes your brand. To become a true thought leader, you must stop relying on reposting others' content and start sharing **your own ideas, perspectives, and expertise.**

I admit it – I was guilty of this myself. If you dig into my YouTube channel, especially around 2018, you'll find that I was reposting motivational mixes and university speeches from the likes of **Robin Williams, Jim Carrey,** and **Les Brown.** I thought I was inspiring people, but in reality, I was just regurgitating what was already out there. Then one day, a well-meaning LinkedIn influencer took me aside for a coffee and gave me some blunt, but much-needed feedback. He said, *"Cullen, your content is engaging, but do you know what its main problem is? **You're not in it!**"* That last part hit me like a ton of bricks. It was a revelation. I had been hiding behind others' content instead of stepping forward with my own voice.

That conversation changed everything for me. I realized that if I wanted to be a trusted voice and build genuine influence, I had to create **original, value-driven content** that reflected my unique insights, not just someone else's.

Avoid clickbait like the plague. It's tempting because it promises quick engagement, but it cheapens your credibility in the long run. Research shows that audiences, particularly on platforms like LinkedIn, are drawn to authenticity. In a world overwhelmed by digital noise, the most impactful voices are the ones who bring real, **original value** consistently. This is where **authenticity** trumps virality every time. As marketing expert **Seth Godin** once said, *"People do not buy goods and services. They buy relationships, stories, and magic."* In the realm of LinkedIn, your story is your currency—make sure it's **yours.**

Consistency and repetition aren't just buzzwords —they're atomic habits that lead to mastery. Just as **James Clear** highlights in his book *Atomic Habits,* small, consistent actions compound into powerful outcomes over time. The same principle applies to building your personal brand. Repeated efforts to engage, provide value, and show up authentically will unlock new opportunities and deeper connections. This isn't about making a one-time impression; it's about building **ongoing trust** and **long-lasting impact**.

Remember, **repetition and consistency** are the keys that unlock success. So, keep showing up, keep being you, and let your steady presence build a path to influence and success.

LinkedIn Judgment: "Use Shock Sparingly" –
A Lesson from John Cleese

During my time as a Guest Experience Manager at the Four Seasons Hotel Sydney, I had the unforgettable experience of hosting John Cleese. After his stay, he invited a few of us to dinner, and I couldn't resist asking him what the best piece of advice he ever received was. With his signature humor and insight, he simply said, *"Use shock sparingly."*

This advice translates perfectly to the world of LinkedIn and content creation, particularly when it comes to the temptation of clickbait. Just like shock in comedy, clickbait might grab attention in the short term, but overuse weakens its effectiveness and damages your credibility. On LinkedIn, the key is not to rely on sensationalism or misleading headlines to draw people in. Instead, focus on delivering real value with your content—authenticity, thoughtful insights, and meaningful engagement. Shock, like clickbait, can get people to click, but it's the depth of your message that will keep them engaged and coming back for more.

Cleese's advice reminds us that while dramatic hooks have their place, it's how you follow up that really matters.

Closing Thoughts: The Magic of Consistency

As we wrap up this exploration of repetition and consistency, let's take a moment to reflect on the magic that happens when you commit to a routine. Picture a small seed planted in fertile soil. With consistent watering and sunlight, it eventually sprouts, grows, and flourishes into something magnificent. The same principle applies to your presence on LinkedIn and beyond.

Every post, every quote, and every interaction you nurture builds upon the last, creating a lush tapestry of engagement and connection. You might feel like you're just shouting into the void at first but remember that every whisper contributes to a symphony. Just as John C. Maxwell wisely noted, small disciplines, repeated every day, lead to greatness over time. So, embrace the journey—each step, no matter how small, is progress.

And let's not forget the joy of sharing your unique voice with the world! Your authenticity is your superpower. When you post with purpose and passion, you invite your audience into your world, sparking conversations that matter. So, when in doubt, lean into your story. Be the beacon of inspiration that you wish to see in others.

Now, as you embark on this consistency quest, keep in mind that it's okay to pivot and adapt along the way. After all, your journey is uniquely yours. Let your audience know that you're in it with them—not just sharing content but sharing a piece of yourself. And trust me, they'll appreciate it more than you realize.

In the end, remember consistency is not just about the content; it's about connection. Every time you hit *"post,"* you're planting a seed that could bloom into a lasting relationship, a valuable insight, or even an unexpected opportunity. So go ahead, unlock those doors with your key of repetition. Show up, shine bright, and let your presence resonate!

Now, get out there and make it count! 💪💎

Law #5 – ABC: Always Be Connecting

Contacts equals contracts. Interactions equals transactions.
— Grant Cardone

This is my spin on the infamous Always Be Closing. You may have seen or heard of it in the intense dramedy *Glengarry Glen Ross*. If you haven't, I highly recommend you watch the scene on YouTube. Alec Baldwin, looking sharp in a business suit and expensive watch, storms into a room full of underperforming salespeople. Well, underperforming is an understatement. The 4 most useless salespeople in the country are in that room. He points to *"ABC"* on the whiteboard – *"Always Be Closing."* While I agree that closing is important, connecting with and growing your network is even more crucial. Without a strong network, you can't expand your net worth. You want a robust sales pipeline so full that when clients leave, drop off or cancel a meeting, it's a relief because you have plenty of business. Luckily, I have a bulletproof strategy for that, too.

Observing the Law – Make it Personal

When I started my LinkedIn journey, I had just 500 connections. After refining my connection approach over six years, I've optimised the message to weapons grade persuasion level. This method has helped me to grow to 23,000 genuine, mostly legal, connections and followers.

A Bulletproof Message

Here's my cold connection request template. I use it when I don't necessarily know the person but have seen them in a recent article, at an event, or elsewhere:

"Hi [1a] [Insert what content or event you've seen them in]
[1b] Hope you're staying safe in the current world order.
[1c] It's great we have so many shared connections like [mention someone's name]
[1d] I would very much like to add you to my network because [reason]
[1e] Looking forward to learning from your updates
[1f] Thank you in advance
Be Great
Cullen/CPH"

Why This Verbiage Works: -

[1a] Tailoring the message to a recent post or event flattered the recipient and acknowledges their work.

[1b] *"Current world order"* is deliberately broad, allowing the recipient to fill in the context based on their experience.

[1c] Mentioning shared connections leverages the law of familiarity and helps to create a sense of common ground.

[1d] The word *"because"* is a powerful persuader. Research by Ellen Langer shows that simply giving a reason, even a minimal one significantly increases compliance. If you don't know what to put, I usually say *"...because I'd be honoured to be part of yours."*

[1e] Expressing interest in their content builds rapport and sets a positive tone for the relationship.

[1f] Thanking in advance assumes acceptance and adds a polite touch.

Here's how I approach messages when I come across a great article in the *AFR* or *Lawyers Weekly*

:

Congrats on article/event

> *"Hi*
> *[2a] Very illuminating article in the LW about _____ - Kudos!*
> *It's great we have so many shared connections like [mention someone's name]*
> *I would very much like to add you to my network because [reason]*
> *Looking forward to learning from your updates*
> *Thank you in advance*
> *Be Great*
> *Cullen/CPH"*

You can even use this one when someone engages on a post you've recently dropped on LinkedIn.

Variation for Engagement

> *"Hi*
> *[3a] Thanks so much for engaging on my post. Really appreciate your insights*
> *It's great we have so many shared connections like [mention someone's name]*
> *I would very much like to add you to my network because [reason]*
> *Looking forward to learning from your updates*

Thank you in advance
Be Great
Cullen/CPH

Why This Works:

- [2a] Complimenting a recent article or engagement acknowledges their effort and builds a connection.
- [3a] Appreciating engagement on your post makes them feel valued and more likely to reciprocate.

LinkedIn Judgement – Connection Alchemy:
Familiarity & Reciprocity

Why do these connection requests work 100% of the time, 90% of the time? Because they play on two important human philosophies: the law of familiarity and the law of reciprocity.

Now let's take a dive deep into the psychological triggers behind these messages.

Breaking Down the Message

[1a] Tailoring your message to specific content flatters the recipient and appeals to their ego and may humble them that you've taken the time to appreciate their content. The same goes for [2a] as well.

[1b] Contextual sensitivity is very powerful when using *"Current world order."* It's a reference to everything and anything. From the pandemic, rising rates, economy etc. It's deliberately left vague because the person

can fill in the gap themselves. based upon the idiom they're living in. Don't fill it in for them.

[1c] When you call out that you both have the same shared connections, the law of familiarity is lurking underneath and because no one wants to be seen to be rude or unkind to a mutual connection, God forbid word would get back to them. Even better, when you have a smaller network, call out the person you know. That makes it more personal and familiar.

[1d] The word *"because"* is a very powerful persuader. As previously mentioned, in a *Harvard study in 1978*, researcher Ellen Langer was in a photocopier queue at a library. In the first trial, she skips the line, goes to the front of the queue, and says, *"Can I please go to the front?"* 60% of people say yes.

In the 2nd trial, when she proclaims, *"Can I go to the front, because I'm in a hurry to get to the doctors,"* 94% of people said yes.

What's most interesting is in the 3rd trial, where the Langer goes to the front of the queue and asks, *"May I cut in front, because I need to make some copies"* a whopping 93% of people still said yes.

So why did this work? It's because the word *"because"* taps into the emotional decision-making and justifies one's reason succinctly. It's almost automatic behaviour; automatic compliance. The human mind only needs to hear *"because,"* and most people accept whatever follows because we also don't believe anyone would lie to us. We are very altruistic in that sense.

So, what does that mean for your LinkedIn game? When the stakes are low, people will opt for the compliant automatic behaviour. If your request is small stakes, and low risk, you should follow your request with *"because"* and give a reason – any reason at all. If the stakes are increasingly high, there may be more resistance, but still not too much.

[1e] Showing that person you'll be looking out for their content and learning from it is a massive rapport builder and sets a positive tone for the relationship to come.

[1f] Thank you in advance, is simple. Begin with the end in mind that you're already connected. It creates an assumption of acceptance and adds a courteous touch.

Transgressing the Law

I've seen may connection requests in my time, many go straight in for the close, which can be off-putting. Here are some of the worst openers:

> *"Do you need leads?"*
> *"How many new clients can you handle?"*
> *"Hello"*
> *"What do you do?"*

All erroneous. These approaches often feel impersonal, stilted and spammy.

Pro Tip #1 – Do Some Research

Whatever you do, when it comes to the world of LinkedIn, a cardinal sin is asking someone what they do. Why? Because it's LinkedIn, and it's readily available on their profile. Such a question feels generic, impersonal, and can come off as disinterested. Asking also seems very odd and spammy, like *"where are you from?"* That's usually blacklisted too.

LinkedIn Judgement - Cultivating Connections: How to Grow Your LinkedIn Network

A connection request is a little seed – you're planting it, not expecting the entire tree to grow immediately. Many people poison the tree, roots and all, as they try and plant the whole damn tree right there and then and expect it to grow. They overcomplicate the process and expect too much too soon.

Use these strategies thoughtfully, and you'll see your connection count soar! I went from 500 to 23,000.

Pro Tip #2 – Personalise Your Connection Requests

Avoid sending generic connection requests. Don't connect without having a message RE do not spray and pray; do not run and gun, avoid mass-connecting without personalization. Which may have been the go-to back in the day to get 100,000's of connections. A well-crafted, personalised message is far more effective and less likely to land you in LinkedIn Jail – a place you definitely don't want to be.

LinkedIn Jail

LinkedIn Jail is a term for when the platform restricts your ability to add new connections, often due to excessive generic requests. In this state, your connection requests may revert back to 'connect' and not be processed. Do not pass go. Do not collect 200 connections.

In the grand tapestry of LinkedIn, every connection is a thread that weaves your network into a powerful supportive fabric. So, remember this: Always Be Connecting, because every new link (no matter if they're your ideal client or not) strengthens your network and every conversation opens new doors. Keep the connections flowing, and watch your professional world expand.

Closing Thoughts: The Power of Connection

In the game of professional networking, the importance of connection cannot be overstated. Think of it this way: every person you connect with is not just a name on a list; they are a potential ally, collaborator, or source of inspiration. As we navigate our careers, it's vital to remember the simple yet profound truth: **your network is your net worth**.

When I look back at my journey from a mere 500 connections to a flourishing community of over 23,000, I see more than just numbers. I see opportunities—doors that opened because I chose to reach out, engage, and connect. Each interaction, no matter how small, has the potential to lead to something remarkable. So, the next time you find yourself hesitating to send that connection request or draft that message, remember this: **Every connection you make is a step toward building a more powerful, expansive, and rewarding network.**

Imagine the ripple effect of your connections. Each new relationship can lead to new insights, referrals, and collaborations that enhance not only your career but the careers of those around you. Think about the person who might be searching for exactly what you offer or the one whose skills perfectly complement yours. By consistently cultivating your network, you're not just investing in yourself; you're contributing to a community where everyone can thrive.

So, as you move forward, let *"Always Be Connecting"* be your mantra. Keep your eyes open for opportunities to engage, share, and learn from others. With every connection, you're planting a seed—one that has the potential to grow into something extraordinary. Every connection is an opportunity—whether it's for a collaboration, referral, or inspiration. Don't hesitate to reach out, engage, and make meaningful connections. The world is a vast, interconnected web of possibilities, and you hold the key to unlocking them.

Now, go out there and connect like your professional life depends on it—because, in many ways, it does. The relationships you nurture today could very well be the foundation of your successes tomorrow. Let's build that network, one meaningful connection at a time!

Law #6 – Celebrate Good Times, Come On!

The more you praise and celebrate your life,
the more there is in life to celebrate.
— Oprah Winfrey

Human beings thrive on celebration. They love it—especially when it's about them. One of my late great teachers, Abraham Maslow, famously introduced his **Hierarchy of Needs**, which outlines the essential requirements for human fulfillment:

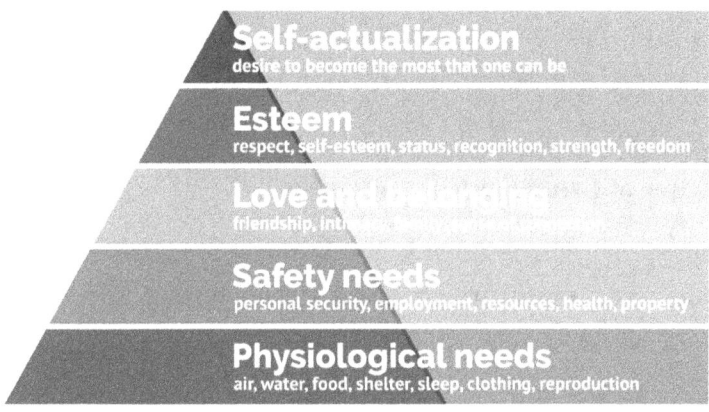

Maslow's Hierarchy of Needs

This five-level pyramid illustrates various needs, in order of importance and necessity to human well-being:

- **Physiological Needs:** At the base of the pyramid are basic needs like food, shelter, and water. These are the foundational elements required for survival.

- **Safety Needs**: The next level encompasses needs such as security, employment, and good health—essentials for stability and comfort.
- **Love and Belonging**: At the centre of the pyramid, ironically the heart, lies the need for friendship, intimacy, family, and a sense of connection. This level emphasizes the importance of relationships in our lives.
- **Esteem**: The second-highest need includes self-esteem, status, recognition, strength, and freedom. It's about how we perceive ourselves and how we want others to perceive us.
- **Self-Actualization**: At the very summit—and my favourite—is the desire to be the best version of oneself, realizing one's potential and pursuing personal growth.

The Power of Esteem in Connection

Esteem is especially relevant to this law. It encompasses our need for recognition and respect, which can profoundly impact our relationships, both online and offline. Research shows that acknowledgment can lead to increased motivation and a sense of belonging. According to a study published in the *Journal of Personality and Social Psychology*, receiving recognition not only boosts self-esteem but also enhances overall well-being, highlighting our innate desire to feel valued and appreciated.

Recognizing others is one of the most powerful ways we can connect as human beings. It lets people know you see them. They exist; they're here! In fact, some of my most successful LinkedIn strategies centre around celebrating others' achievements. During Awards and Promotions season, I find this is the most effective time to connect with someone. Why? Because when someone shares a humble brag about their accomplishments, they're not just sharing information; they're opening themselves up to acknowledgment and flattery.

A Moment of Recognition

Let me share a personal experience. Last year, I noticed a colleague from my old high school, haven't spoken in 20 years, post about a significant career promotion. Rather than merely likely the post, I took the time to leave a thoughtful comment, expressing how proud I was of their achievement. Within minutes, they responded with gratitude, and we began a conversation that rekindled our connection. This simple act of recognition not only made their day but also re-established our professional relationship, leading to collaborative opportunities down the line. We actually just did their home loan.

Everyone wants to feel important, so make it a point to celebrate their accomplishments and make them feel seen. Whether it's through a comment, a personalized message, or a share, your acknowledgment can foster meaningful connections and elevate your professional network. After all, when you contribute to someone else's sense of esteem, you enhance your own influence and presence in their eyes—and in the broader LinkedIn community.

Observing the Law

When I first started working with lawyers, I noticed something unique about their profession. Prestige and acclaim are paramount. Just imagine, these lawyers, especially those in top tier law, are the smartest people at high school, usually with ATAR's of 99.9 and now working for the elite of the elite. And they continue to seek validation. So, how do they showcase their ongoing success to their peers?

A good old fashioned humble brag on LinkedIn of course!

Oh, you think I'm joking? Wait until the *Lawyers Weekly* announces the winners of one of their awards nights of nights; you can count on two things: -

1) A LinkedIn post with a photo of the award recipient
2) Text expressing feigned humility, often with phrases like *"I'm so humbled"* or *"Team effort"*

Ironically (and amusingly), many of these awards are self-nominated, emphasising the importance of recognition even further. Be mindful that some firms will even write on behalf of the award winner, adding pithy remarks like *"I won...so shocked!"* Which always makes me smile.

Here's my bulletproof connection message to send to members of your tribe when you've seen they've won an award (and indeed finalists too, can't forget them). I'll start with the latter first. This is assuming you're not connected. Note best to send before the award ceremony (1-2 days usually go out so it's nice and fresh):

Before the Award Ceremony - Best of Luck

> *"Hi*
> *Best of luck in the [Name of awards]* ✌
> *Hope you're staying safe in the current world order.*

> *I would very much like to add you to my network because I'd be honoured to be part of yours. Looking forward to learning from your updates. Be Great*
> *Cullen"*

After Winning - Congrats (Day after winning)

> *"Hi*
> *Congrats on taking out [Name of award]* 🏆
> *Hope you're staying safe in the current world order.*
> *I would very much like to add you to my network because I'd be honoured to be part of yours. Looking forward to learning from your updates. Be Great*
> *Cullen"*

Pro Tip #1 – Go Down The List:

When you find and awards ceremony where many of your connections are nominated, download the list from the event's website and methodically add the finalists on LinkedIn using the above connection messages. Again, best to do so before the event and give yourself a couple of days to at least a week to give people time to respond. And follow up Finalists and Winners of the event, 1-2 days after their triumph. so nice and fresh.

Pro Tip #2 – Mention the Award 🏆

Always mention the exact name of the award. It shows you've done your homework and aren't just sending blanket messages out.

Pro Tip #3 – Stay Out of LinkedIn Jail

If there are several finalists, to ensure you're not picked up by the LinkedIn Police, be sure to change up your message by moving the congrats from the top of the message to the bottom. Other quirky yet effective methods are simply changing *"Hey"* to *"Hi"* or *"Good Evening."* Maybe even change up your sign off. All the best etc. Even your name as well. I sometimes sign off as CPH

Believe me, the LinkedIn police can spot when your messages look like they're repeating as it looks like spam. You don't want to be thrown in LinkedIn Jail! It's a real place.

Pro Tip #4 – Moving On Up

Apply the same approach to promotions. As mentioned before, in law, the hierarchy is very similar to banking, my background, and it's important to celebrate your rise to the next level. Play on this highly stratified infrastructure and people's need to feel important. Celebrate advancements like making Partner or Special Counsel, as these are significant milestones. LinkedIn makes messaging promotees very easy by putting all recently promoted under 'My Network' –> Catch Up à 'Promotions' (This feature as of 2024 has recently been updated)

> *"Hi*
> *Congrats on the recent promotion to [Position]*
> *Hope you're staying safe in the current world order.*
> *I would very much like to add you to my network because I'd*

be honoured to be part of yours. Looking forward to learning from your updates. Be Great
Cullen"

Pro Tip #5 – Note The Position

Understanding the significance of the position is crucial. For instance, in law, making special counsel often required 10 years of service; while becoming or Making Partner is 15-20 years which is a huge achievement. It's very important to know where people sit so tailor your message accordingly.

Pro Tip #6 – Subscribe to Your Tribe's Newsletter or Website

I know lawyers read and respect *Lawyers Weekly* with over 100,000 subscribers for their online newsletter. Here they share industry discussions, awards, promotions, podcasts, interviews, partners etc. so I make a point to connect and reach out to anyone featured to congratulate them on a job well done. I hit my 20-person daily connection goal I set myself simply by going through my daily *Lawyers Weekly* emails (I get 4-5 a day). I also go through the AFR and do the same. So do some research, find a newsletter or medium your tribe all gravitate towards and share that love. Here's my connection request for those features: -

> *"Hi*
> *Cracking article in the Lawyers Weekly – I really enjoyed [something specific about article]*
> *Hope you're staying safe in the current world order.*

> *I would very much like to add you to my network because I'd be honoured to be part of yours. Looking forward to learning from your updates. Be Great*
> *Cullen"*

Be sure to note where you saw them and what you liked, shows you did your homework and genuinely appreciated what they put forward. Some are being interviewed for the first time, so they'll really boost you in their esteem if you give them positive feedback.

LinkedIn Judgement – Power is a Corporate Ladder

Everyone wants to feel important. The current corporate arena mirrors the power dynamics of the old aristocratic court; nobody seeks less power; everybody desires more. And those that downplay their ambitions are often the most adept players of the game.

In the old court, courtiers sought proximity to the power source - The Queen or King. In business, it's about ascending to roles like Managing Partner or CEO as quickly and efficiently as possible.

The meritocracy in professions like law & banking values both excellence and tenure.

Here's a general guide for career progression:

- 0-1 Years: Graduate
- 1-5 Years: Associate
- 5-10 Years: Senior Associate
- 10-15 Years: Special Counsel/Associate Director

- 15-20 Years: Salaried Partner/Division Head
- 20-25 Years: Equity Partner/Banking Head

*The above is only a rough guide and there are, of course, many exceptions and outliers in career projection.

This is the general rule for any profession. The more years put in, the more esteem, acclaim, and opportunity one is given.

Why is the above important? The next time you see a promotion on LinkedIn, spare a thought for the years that person has invested & sacrificed in their life to get where they are. If you spare that extra thought before leaving your VM message, you may put a bit more effort into your next one.

By acknowledging their achievements, you show respect for their journey and contributions.

So, keep this in mind as you go about your LinkedIn journey: just like Kool & The Gang's catchy tune says, *"Celebrate good times, come one!"* Remember, it's not just about the big wins but also the little victories. Recognize and celebrate those moments – both yours and others. By doing so, you'll find that success and connections multiply. After all, the rhythm of recognition and celebration is the heartbeat of thriving on LinkedIn. Now go on, turn up the volume and let the celebration begin!

Closing Thoughts – Celebrate to Elevate

In the grand tapestry of our professional lives, every thread counts. Each achievement, no matter how small, contributes to the vibrant picture of who we are and what we strive for. As Oprah Winfrey's powerful mantra goes, *"The more you praise and celebrate your life, the more there is in life to celebrate."* This law underscores the significance of celebration—not merely as a momentary joy but as a strategic tool for growth and connection.

When you celebrate the achievements of others, you're not just acknowledging their hard work; you're actively participating in a culture of support and recognition. In doing so, you amplify your influence, strengthen your network, and foster an environment where everyone can thrive. Whether it's a simple congratulatory message or a heartfelt comment on a post, your acknowledgment can spark meaningful conversations and rekindle relationships that may have faded over time.

As you navigate your LinkedIn journey, remember that every interaction is an opportunity to celebrate. Recognize the milestones of your colleagues, friends, and even acquaintances. A simple gesture can make a world of difference, transforming fleeting connections into lasting partnerships.

The corporate landscape may resemble a game of thrones but remember this: true power lies in uplifting those around you. When we elevate others, we elevate ourselves. So, take a moment to turn up the volume, play that infectious tune, and celebrate good times—yours and others. By doing so, you not only enrich your professional experience but also contribute to a thriving community that celebrates success in all its forms.

Now, let's take this rhythm of recognition into action. Go out there, connect, and let the celebrations begin!

Law #7 – Leave a Message, After the Tone

*The key to success is to find a way to stand out — to be
a purple cow in a field of monochrome Holsteins.*
— Seth Godin

So, you've connected with your first tribe of followers, and they've accepted your connection request. Now what?

If you're like many LinkedIn users, you'll fall into one of two categories: either you do nothing (which is the most common response) or, as I was guilty of in my early days, you dive into a sales pitch. Here's a blast from my past - our old **Frankenstein** message we used early on we started our LinkedIn journey:

> Thank you for the connect, trust all is well. As a partner at a leading firm, I'm sure that you are extremely busy looking after your clients. We understand, we deal with professionals like yourself on a daily basis. We know the pace that you're no doubt working to as Legal Home Loans is the first and only finance company in Australia specialising in bespoke finance solutions tailored for elite legal professionals. We see that many of our clients of similar status find managing their home & investment loans both time consuming and laborious.
>
> Our job is to make this convoluted process seamless having minimal impact on your day to day whilst knowing that your lending is competitive and that there is someone you can

easily contact with any ongoing queries. In light of recent rate rises at 3 of the 4 major banks, now may be the ideal time to review current structures as well as have our team manage your accounts going forward. You are likely eligible for lawyer specific benefits when dealing with certain banks that you haven't been made aware of previously.

We would be delighted to meet you for a 30-minute meeting at your office to discuss further so please let me know when would best suit? Look forward to hearing from you. Best regards Cullen T: 0499 913 930 E: c.haynes@legalhomeloans.com.au W: www.legalhomeloans.com.au As featured in *Lawyers Weekly* https://www.lawyersweekly.com.au/partner-features/24007-finally-a-dedicated-finance-broker-for-lawyers

Wow, talk about a lot to digest, right? While this may read very professional some, it is quite the block of literature, right there, and for every 100 messages, I got only 10 providing some response and, at best, 1 meeting. We called it the *"Frankenstein message,"* because it combined all elements, we thought made our offering world-class. While I do not advocate still using it as a means to connect, I will say, some of our first clients came on board with it. But many opportunities were missed I'd wager.

There is a far better way that most people don't know about, dear reader, that will take your connection rate, follow up coffees/ meetings, and your LinkedIn game generally, to the next level.

Enter the VM feature.

What? Never heard of it. That's likely because you've been too busy sliding into DMs to notice the little microphone symbol in the bottom right-hand corner. This hidden gem is one of the most powerful tools on LinkedIn and will set you apart from 99% of users. 🎤

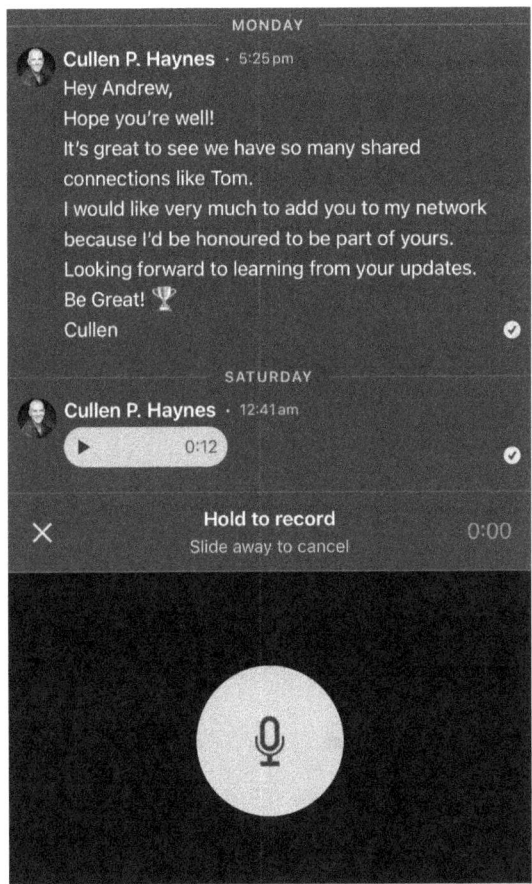

LinkedIn's Voicemail Feature/Button

It's simple, after someone has accepted, hold down the mic symbol, record a 10-20 second VM and watch your tribe grow and engage!

Pro Tip #1 – Keep It Short

If someone receives a 1-minute message, they may be less inclined to stay and listen. 10-20 seconds is short and punchy and more likely to cause someone to click and engage. Aim for brevity and clarity to enhance engagement.

Observing the Law

The voicemail that wows! This has been fine-tuned over years of experimentation and leverages psychological principles we've already discussed.

There are three parts to this message:

> "Hi [Use name]
> 1) Thank you so much for the connection. I truly value it.
> 2) If you're not against it, would love to catch up for a coffee when you're next in the CBD, it's on me <u>because</u> I'm a big believer in taking the online offline. Let me know if this week or next week works?
> 3) By the way, we've recently come out with our latest article in the Lawyers Weekly so let me know if you'd like me to send your way because it's on the latest rate rise
> Looking forward to seeing your posts. Be well."

You'll get one of 3 reactions to this message if they don't respond immediately (sometimes it takes time):

1) "OMG you're the first voicemail I've received. How did you do that?" OR "Didn't know that was a thing!"

2) *"I'd love to meet for coffee. Where and when?"*
3) *"Yes, please send me your article"*

Each of these represents great engagement because they're so different. Let's go through the 3 parts of the message:

1) **Surprise and Delight**: Most people aren't used to receiving voicemails, making it a unique and memorable experience.
2) **Personal Connection**: Offering coffee fosters personal interaction, moving the relationship offline and deeper. Face to face belly to belly. And most Sydneysiders love a good coffee and one where you're willing to meet at their favourite spot. Less formal and salesy.
3) **Expertise and Value:** This is what's called permission-based sales and shows that you're a subject matter expert in a medium that they recognise and respect. People will think of you when they think of your service.

The Law in Effect (Part 1)

The Laws of LinkedIn

The Law in Effect (Part 2)

LinkedIn Judgement – The Voicemail That Pops: Be the Purple Cow

This Voicemail is a Purple Cow. Why? Well as Seth Godin most famously said, in a field of cows, you'll always notice the purple one, because it's unique, different, and striking. The VM is also refreshing as you've taken the time to record it just for that person. It cannot be duplicated or outsourced, so you will not be picked up by the LinkedIn police either.

Also, it's authentic and genuine and non-salesy. Be the Purple Cow - record your first message and stand out.

Transgressing the Law

Now #NoJudgement, as I've been guilty of this too in my early LinkedIn days. But like a gawky child star who falls out of the spotlight, it gets old very fast. Many of you are familiar with receiving *"The Block"* or *"Pitch Slap"* as I call it. The large garish chunk of text that smells like selling and spam. People want to be bought not sold. They want to be wooed and to dance, at least feigning it. Buy me dinner or coffee first at least. It usually says "Do you need a VA, options here…" *Goes on for 20-30 lines more. People prefer to build a relationship before committing.

Avoid these overly aggressive approaches. You're better than that, dear reader. Circling back to our original Frankenstein message. It was crafted with good intentions it lacked that personal touch voice offers. Together with my business partner, I wrote it back in the day. We were in an office in mid-2018 (the year we started) with another legend of LinkedIn, Dom Nesci, and wanted to put together the perfect message with the right elements to entice our tribe. And we compared, moulded, and came up with our Frankenstein from many parts. Looking back, not a bad message, however, not as powerful as a personalised voice message that is non-threatening, engaging and authentic.

Six years later, I still get responses to this message, and people reaching out wanting loans, so I'm not saying it doesn't work sometimes. And I met with some very prominent Partners and Barristers (The crème de la crème of our client base) that I had no business seeing at that time; some of which are now clients and good friends to this day. Shout out to this #LegendOfLaw Norman Ayoub, one of the kindest lawyers I know who is also a bustling shoe seller. Check out his page here:

https://www.instagram.com/thesoleemporium/?hl=en

The message I want you to walk away with, here, is that I know many opportunities were closed to me because I took the Frankenstein message approach. As my Pa is fond of saying *"A stopped clock is right twice a day."* I would have had more meaningful conversations over offer, off the back of an impactful voicemail.

Try it out for yourself and see the difference.

In a world awash with LinkedIn pitches that blend into a sea of sameness, your voicemail can be the purple cow that stands out. While the Frankenstein messages of the past had their place, it's the personal touch of a short, genuine voicemail that will make you memorable.

So next time you connect, don't just send another generic message—record a voicemail that shows you've taken the time to truly engage. After all, it's not just about sending messages; it's about making connections that resonate.

As you hit that record button, remember this:

"The best way to predict the future is to create it." — *Peter Drucker*

Be the creator of your LinkedIn success story. Stand out, be genuine, and let your voice be the one they remember.

Hit record and let your LinkedIn game change—one voicemail at a time.

Be the Purple Cow

Closing Thoughts: Be the Purple Cow, Not the Frankenstein

So, you've made it this far. You've learned about the Frankenstein message of yesteryear, laughed at its blocky awkwardness, and discovered the untapped magic of the LinkedIn voicemail feature. It's like stumbling across a superpower no one else knows they have. But the question is, will you use it?

Think of every connection as an opportunity—not to push your services, but to build something authentic. Seth Godin nailed it: in a field of white and black Holsteins, you want to be that Purple Cow. It's not about blending in; it's about standing out, and doing so with sincerity, not sales pitches.

The Frankenstein approach may have gotten me a few clients back in the day, but I missed out on so many more. A voicemail—personal, quick, and genuine—could have made all the difference. Today, you're armed with the secret weapon to transform those cold connections into warm relationships.

So, next time you find yourself staring at the LinkedIn message box, tempted to send another generic message, be bold, be brave, and hit that microphone icon. Surprise and delight your audience with the power of your own voice.

After all, it's the small, thoughtful gestures that create the most lasting impact.

Ready to be the Purple Cow?

Law #8 – Start an Entourage: Turn on Creator Mode

Choose to lead, and gain the choice of the follower.
— Michael Dooley

"If you build it, they will come." This is one of my favorite movie quotes, as quoted by my dear friend Darren Mort, Legend of Law and Barrister, during one of our LawLive's. It comes from the iconic film *Field of Dreams* with Kevin Costner. But what's this '80s movie, which may elicit an eye roll, have to do with a book on LinkedIn growth? In the realm of LinkedIn, the default Connect Mode does not, in my opinion, provide the necessary infrastructure to scale effectively and attract or engage your ideal followers.

The alternative I highly advocate is Creator Mode, allowing people to follow you with one click.

Humans are lazy creatures and naturally inclined to take the easier path. In Connect Mode, to have someone follow you, they either need to:

- Press *"Connect"* (Unlikely – unless they're in marketing or abroad)
- Click on the 3 dots next to your profile, then click *"Follow"* (Even more unlikely)

So, with those things in mind, what can you do to make it easier? Turn on Creator Mode, of course!

By turning on Creator Mode, you transform your LinkedIn experience in three key ways:

1) **Simplify Following:** Creator Mode turns the *"Connect"* button into a *"Follow"* button, making it easier for people to follow you without sending a connection request. This frictionless option boosts your follower count.
2) **Showcase Your Niche:** Creator Mode lets you display up to five hashtags that define your niche, ensuring your audience immediately understands your areas of expertise.
3) **Visible Followers:** Your follower count is displayed prominently, starting at 500. This visible social proof can attract even more followers, since people are drawn to accounts with a strong following. So now, let me ask you again. Are you more likely to follow someone with Creator Mode turned on or off? I think you know the answer to that.

Observing the Law

For those in the legal profession, my tribe, privacy is often a priority. Yet, there are standout professionals who embrace visibility and use it to their advantage; they're truly diamonds in the rough. Follow these #LegendsOfLaw who excel with Creator Mode:

- Alistair Marshall
- Clarissa Rayward
- David Gale
- Darren Mort
- Harry Cormack
- Jahan Kalantir

- James d'Apice
- Jason Symons
- Lara Wentworth
- Nicole Davidson
- Pepe Kish
- Peter Hunt
- Reena Strehle
- Stefanie Costi

Leading (or following) profiles by example

These professionals exemplify how turning on Creator Mode can enhance your LinkedIn presence, allowing you to build a more engaged and responsive audience.

Transgressing the Law

Here's a true story. I once tried to connect with a lawyer on LinkedIn who responded with:

> *"I'm sorry Cullen, I'm saying no, because I don't connect with anyone I don't know."*

We've still not connected to this day. Her follower/connection count was a mere 17. This response is a classic example of a missed opportunity. As Tony Robbins wisely said, *"If you always do what you've always done, you'll always get what you've always gotten."*

This experience contrasts sharply with what research suggests on professional relationships. A study conducted by the *Harvard Business Review* found that professionals with larger and more diverse networks tend to develop more innovative ideas and have faster career advancement. The study emphasized that networks with *"non-redundant"* ties, meaning connections outside your usual circles, often offer access to information and opportunities that would otherwise be out of reach. It turns out that when we limit ourselves to people we already know, we close off access to a wider range of resources and knowledge.

Additionally, a *University of Virginia* study on the effects of online networking revealed that those who frequently engage with new people outside their immediate circles are more likely to experience professional growth and develop a higher level of job satisfaction. LinkedIn, being one of the largest professional platforms globally, provides an unprecedented opportunity to cultivate these weak ties and expand your network beyond your immediate familiarity.

By only connecting with people you know, you're essentially shutting the door on potential mentors, collaborators, and future opportunities. So, don't be like this lawyer. Be open, embrace new connections, and build relationships that could expand your knowledge, influence, and opportunities.

Don't be like this lawyer, please!

LinkedIn Judgement - Creator Mode: A Tool for Growth, Not a Quick Fix

Turning on Creator Mode is not a magic bullet; it's just one tool in your LinkedIn toolbox. Building a meaningful following requires more than just switching modes. You still need to be someone who works and earns their following.

That comes through time, consistent effort and engagement. Or as my man, Red, in *The Shawshank Redemption* says when it comes to making diamonds, *"Pressure and Time."* Let's aim for diamonds without the pressure, shall we? 😄

Building a tribe takes time. Your audience needs to become familiar with your content and understand who you are and what you stand for. Heck, if you're starting from scratch, like many of you, dear readers, it will even more time for you to adapt to your new posting routine.

James Clear in his book *Atomic Habits* emphasises that the 21-day mark is crucial for forming a last habit. If you consistently post every day for 21 days, watch how people react on the 22nd day if you suddenly stop. They might start wondering whether you're okay. Where did you go? It's thrilling to know that your tribe depends on your posts as part of their routine. Imagine the influence you can wield with your content.

I recently had a month off for my second baby in September. One of my legal connections left me a voice message and said: -

> *"Cullen, I don't know whether you're not posting or I'm not seeing your posts but just letting you know I'm here if you want to chat. I hope you're okay"*

I let them know immediately that I was fine, and that she was right. I'd only posted 1-2 time per day, sometimes 1-2 in a week, rather than my 3-5 daily habitual posts.

Pro Tip #1 – What Circulates Freely, Loses Value

In LinkedIn posts, oversaturation reduces impact. When something is available too often, it becomes common and loses its specialness. This principle is echoed in Robert Greene's *48 Laws of Power*. Apply this in your posts: avoid lowest common denominator content or clickbait. Instead, focus on adding genuine value with the majority of your content. This approach sets the stage for our next law.

Closing Thoughts – The Spotlight is Yours

So, there you have it— Creator Mode isn't just a feature—it's a bold declaration that you're ready to step into the limelight. It's like stepping onto a stage where your audience is eagerly awaiting, where the curtain rises, and the audience takes their seats, eager to see what you've got to offer. But here's the key: it's not enough to simply stand there. You have to deliver a performance worthy of the applause.

Turning on Creator Mode is the easy part, sustaining your audience's attention and building a loyal following takes effort, consistency, and authenticity. You have to show up, post with purpose, and share insights that genuinely resonate with your audience. As the great Kevin Costner reminds us, *"If you build it, they will come."* But here's the twist—if you build it well, they won't just come; they'll stay.

In the vast theatre of LinkedIn, you have the chance to be more than just another face in the crowd. By embracing Creator Mode, you're signalling to your audience that you're ready to lead, to share, and to build something meaningful. The question is: are you ready to put in the time and effort to keep them engaged?

Remember, your audience isn't looking for just another post; they're looking for leadership, for value, for something that makes them think, smile, or learn. So, as you turn on Creator Mode, don't just think about what you'll post next. Think about the long game—how will you consistently deliver content that keeps your audience coming back for more?

You've got the stage, you've got the spotlight, and now it's time to shine. Your LinkedIn entourage is waiting—are you ready to make your grand entrance?

Law #9 – The 80/20 Rule of Sales (And Life)

The majority of effects come from the minority of causes.
— Vilfredo Pareto

In both business and life, adding value is paramount. Elevation through education. Arnold Schwarzenegger's new book, inspired by his father's advice, is both pithy and eloquent; 'Be Useful'. Gary Vaynerchuk or Gary Vee expands on this with his *"Jab, Jab, Jab, Jab, Right Hook"* strategy. Before making a direct request, focus on providing value. To get the ultimate sale, and knock the sale out as it were, you need to pre-empt with a lead-up to the knockout. You need to be a person who adds value first, then asks for the sale.

Your content should reflect this approach: For every four posts that educate, uplift, and add value, one should be a clear CTA—Call-to-Action: Buy Now, Here's the link. Enter the Pareto Principle…

Understanding the Pareto Principle

The Pareto Principle, also known as the 80/20 rule, states that 80% of effects come from 20% of causes, a concept named after the Italian economist Vilfredo Pareto. This principle is often observed in various domains: 80% of results come from 20% of efforts, 80% of profits come from 20% of customers and so on.

Applying the Pareto Principle

In the context of LinkedIn and content posting, this principle means focusing on how you distribute your content:

- **80% Value-Adding Posts:** These should be educational, uplifting, and designed to engage and provide value to your audience. They help build trust and establish your authority.
- **20% Call-to-Action (CTA) Posts:** These posts are where you make a direct ask, such as promoting a product, service, or special offer. These should be clear and compelling but balanced by the value-adding content to maintain engagement and avoid overwhelming your audience with constant sales pitches. This breaks rapport and trust.

Call-to-Action (CTA)

Apply this principle to your posting frequency. If you post five times a week, ensure your final post of the week (or one of them) is a CTA. Make sure to include a CTA if you post multiple times a day.

Trust that your tribe appreciates CTAs as long as they're preceded by value.

Observing the Law

Grant Cardone, a prominent and polarising sales coach and marketer, exemplifies this principle. Love him, hate him, he's a very interesting personality indeed. Cardone is a Big believer in the concept of *"They won't flow you unless they know you."*

His content is jam packed, even his free events and books like *The 10X Rule* where you 10X your goals and 10X your action. Something which we'll talk about later.

Despite the flood of emails, I received from him daily (5-6), his high-value content—has made me a loyal customer. Your CTA's can take various forms, as long as they're clear and consistent with your brand. For instance, I share anonymous conversations with real clients on LinkedIn, incorporating humour and direct CTAs in my *Meanwhile on Cullen's Sunday Afternoon Call* post. If often includes a funny anecdote or conversation with a client and highlights the exact offer, how to get it and next steps. Humour is a very powerful persuasion tool. This approach resonates with my audience of busy lawyers and reinforces my brand and message. It also shows that I'm speaking with high-profile Partners and Barristers which are usually who I spotlight and are my ideal clientele, most senior in law with the most need for our services.

Many clients in my network love them as it's very me and on brand and talks to busy lawyer life (my tribe). I also do the same thing with my videos. 90% NIL LMI or 10% lending for lawyers was the message when we first started our business, and we still share that message today.

We're currently promoting our **Staff Benefits Program**, which has successfully onboarded over 30% of Big Law firms. Through this initiative, we engage with their employee base 3-4 times a year via our **Mortgage Masterclasses**. Participants gain access to our platinum broking service and receive a $1,000 credit upon settlement of their loan. By leveraging the **Pareto Principle**, we recognize that it's far more efficient at this stage of our business to cultivate Firm Relationships that can yield individual opportunities rather than pursuing those individual opportunities directly.

It's important to repeat your call-to-action multiple times. A recent example of this strategy in action involved filming an engaging video in the stunning offices of Wotton + Kearney, overlooking the harbour. In the video, we not only celebrated the team who hosted us but also shared the numerous benefits of our program:

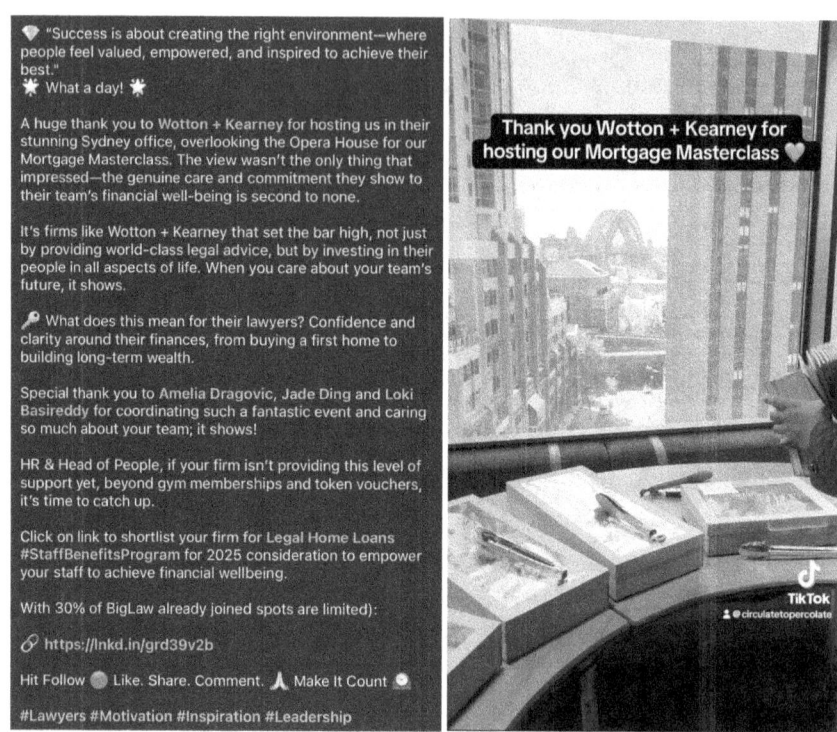

Call to Action Post | LHL Staff Benefits Program Video, Shout Out & Link

Pro Tip #1 – Just a little bit of history repeating

Don't worry about repeating your message. I promise you; your audience will find new value in familiar content, and repetition helps reinforce your message. I've experienced this firsthand. I've repeated the same message for the last 5 years *Lawyers Buy with 10%* and still to this day, I get lawyers who tell me *"I didn't know that they could borrow with as little as 10% deposit with waived mortgage insurance."* That's because there's 88,000 of them and I cannot ever ensure all 88,000 know about it just through one of my posts.

So, keep repeating, it's the best way to drill your message in.

It reminds me of a story I once heard at a Tony Robbins, *Unleash the Power Within* event. He talked about his old pastor who came in on the first Sunday of the month and preached his sermon, which was riveting, powerful and engaging. The second Sunday, he gave the same sermon, people still enjoyed it, but were scratching their heads as it was the same as the Sunday before. The third Sunday? You guessed it, delivered the same sermon.

By the time he reached the last Sunday of the month, some of the senior members of the church pulled the pastor aside and said, *"Father, are you alright? Do you realise you've given the same sermon for the last four Sundays now?"*

The Father gave a nice sincere smile and said, *"Oh you noticed, I'm glad. And I'll keep repeating this sermon until you understand the message and put into practice what I've been talking about"*

Classic!

Transgressing the Law

Avoid the pitfalls of posting only CTAs. Doing so erodes the valuable emotional capital and trust you've built while also alienating your audience. Research from the *Nielsen Global Trust in Advertising study* reveals that 83% of consumers trust recommendations from friends and family over any other form of advertising. This highlights the importance of building genuine relationships through valuable content rather than frequent sales pitches. People love buying valuable things, but they don't want to feel preached or sold to.

I once followed someone who inundated their audience with constant sales posts; their name has since faded from memory, underscoring the lesson: avoid being forgettable by ensuring your posts provide value beyond mere sales pitches. A study conducted by *HubSpot* showed that brands providing useful, educational content see a 60% higher conversion rate than those focused solely on sales. This proves that genuine engagement and value are far more effective in creating lasting connections.

LinkedIn Judgement - It's Not Who You Know, It's Who Knows You: The BBQ Reality Check

One of the most important business lessons I've ever been taught was from my mentor at Macquarie, who told me, *"Cullen, don't be vain, success in this world is not measured by the people you know. It's not who you know, it's who knows you!"*

This insight is profound, it's not your personal connections who make a purchase, but rather those who are aware of what you offer and think of you when they need it.

Recall the common scenario of being at a BBQ and a friend mentions they've just bought a product or service you offer. Ouch! That stings. Knife to the heart. You tell them, you're in that business and they could have got a far more superior deal through you. *"Sorry mate, didn't know you provided that!"*

This experience isn't unusual, and it's not necessarily your friend's for not knowing about your service. It's yours! You must ensure that people know what you do. As David Goggins would say, own it. The only reason someone might choose a competitor (who's most likely inferior to your offering) is that you didn't put yourself out there or make what you do sufficiently memorable to spring to mind when it counts.

So, don't take it personally, put your big boy, big girl, non-binary pants on, go out there and make yourself memorable and valuable. Be the person they turn to next time. Make sure that at the next BBQ, you're the one they think of first, and let your competitors be the ones who find out they missed out.

Pro Tip #2 – Hook, Story, Offer

I learnt this little gem from Russell Brunson, the Click Funnels guy. He teaches that the best marketing Call-To-Action follows three elements: **Hook, Story, Offer**

Hook – Something punchy that grabs attention and pulls your tribe in. It could be a headline or a compelling question: -

> *"Did you know many lawyers are eligible to borrow with just a 10% deposit in NSW?"*

Story – The most powerful tool in your arsenal is storytelling. It taps into emotions, making your message relatable and visual. People remember stories, they make your message stick. Here's a real-life example:

> *"Jennifer, a lawyer in Sydney, was able to purchase her dream home for $1,000,000 and save $20,000 on lender's mortgage insurance using this method."*

Offer – Now that you've captured attention and connected emotionally, the offer is your chance to provide clear, concise information about your product, its value, and how you get it. For instance:

> *Lawyers, buy with just 10% deposit and no LMI. Rates from 5.59% for owner-occupied, exclusive terms with waived mortgage insurance, and up to $3,000 refinance cashback for eligible Law Society members. Leverage your profession, conserve time, and save thousands! Get started today.*

OR What I paste in every comment of my posts on LinkedIn:

> Lawyers, buy with just 10% deposit, no LMI
> ✅ Platinum Broker Certified - Top 1% - Preferential Rates, Turn Around Times & Policies
> ✅ Rates* from 5.59% Owner Occupied
> 🔸 5,79% Investment - P & I
> 🔸 6.34% Investment - Interest Only
> ✅ Exclusive legal credit policy 10% Deposit waived LMI
> ✅ Up to $3,000 Refinance Cash Back
> ✅ $500 Rebate for eligible Law Soc Members
> ✅ Finance solutions for salaried & equity Partners
> ✅ Barristers, 100% Unsecured Chambers
> ✅ Exclusive terms to access Australia's leading Private Banks

Leverage your profession ⚖️ conserve time ⏱ save thousands

🔖 *Subject to individual lending position

Weigh your options while WFH 🏠

⚖️ https://www.legalhomeloans.com.au/contact-us

#Lawyers #HomeLoans

Here's another example of the Hook, Story and Offer which has become a regular approach for me. Usually, a quote to grab the mass audience, the story (and shout out) of our partner firm or client and link to the offer, in this case our Staff Benefits Program targeted at HR teams within Big Law firms:

Hook, Story, Offer at work

Closing Thoughts: The Final Jab

Remember, just like in boxing, the power of a knockout lies in the setup. Your 80% value-driven content is the jab, softening your audience up, keeping them engaged. Then comes the right hook—the Call-to-Action that knocks it out of the park. And if your hook is strong enough, they won't just lean in, they'll act.

But here's the secret: in the game of life, business, and LinkedIn, it's not the loudest shout that wins—it's the consistent whisper. Keep adding value. Keep showing up. And when the time is right, don't hesitate to swing for the fences.

So, throw those jabs, keep your hands up, and when you see the opening—land your CTA with precision. After all, it's not just about selling, it's about serving (service is always senior to sales). And when you serve first, your tribe won't just remember you—they'll come knocking on your door.

Now get out there and jab, jab, jab...right hook! 🥊

Law #10 – Follow Me: Like, Share & Subscribe

Do not go where the path may lead. Go instead, where there is no path, and leave a trail.
— *Ralph Waldo Emerson*

This one's right out of the YouTube playbook; you need to flex that "ask" muscle and encourage people to hit that follow button! You may think you're above asking people to follow you. You may think it's unnecessary, or you're not confident enough to stand by the quality of your content. But if you can't summon the courage to say *"Hey You! Follow me,"* then perhaps you don't want to create a following at all.

I don't claim to be a Bible expert or particularly religious, but there's no denying that Jesus of Nazareth delivered one of the most effective and straightforward calls to action: 'Follow me.'

Observing the Law

Not many people know this, but I'm a big fan of found-footage horror clips. You know the ones—grainy, shaky camera footage where, by the end, the camera breaks, goes dark, or the person filming mysteriously disappears. My guilty pleasure is a YouTuber named Chills, who puts out countdown videos ranking the creepiest, most chilling moments of the week. Apart from his unique, robotic cadence, what stands out is how, right before revealing video #1, he issues a clever challenge: *"Since you've made it this far, why don't you hit that follow button? I release four new videos each week."*

That's brilliant! Chills has gamified the CTA (call-to-action), framing it as a challenge. Instead of a generic plea for subscribers, he makes it feel like a reward for commitment. *"You've already made it through the spookiest moments, so why not take one more step?"* As a result, he has amassed over 6.21 million subscribers as of this writing. If someone with a voice that's polarizing enough to drive some people away can pull it off, then what's stopping you?

The psychology behind Chills' approach mirrors the *foot-in-the-door technique*. This technique, studied by psychologists *Freedman and Fraser in 1966*, shows that people are more likely to agree to a larger request, such as subscribing, after first agreeing to a smaller one, like watching the video. The original study was done with a small stickers *"Be a safe driver"* asked to be placed in select people's homes. A few weeks later, they came back and asked if they could put a big ugly *"Drive carefully"* sign in their front yard. Remarkably, those who agreed to the sticker were 76% more likely to agree. The lesson? Once someone has invested time and attention in your content, they're more likely to reciprocate by hitting that follow button. It's human nature to want to finish what we've started—often referred to as the *consistency principle* in behavioural psychology. Chills leverages this in a way that makes his audience feel part of a journey, which ultimately strengthens engagement.

This strategy doesn't just work for YouTubers. Consider Neil Patel, a leading digital marketer. Neil has built his empire by giving away an incredible amount of free value—guides, tools, insights—before ever making an ask. And when he does ask, whether it's to follow his blog, join his webinar, or purchase a service, the audience is ready and willing, because they've already received so much. He follows a *"give, give, give, ask"* model, mirroring Chills' strategy.

So how can you replicate this on LinkedIn?

Here's my version of the *"Follow Me"* CTA that I use at the end of every post:

> Hit Follow 🎯 Like. Share. Comment. 🙏 Make It Count 🐢
> [Hashtags go here]

Because I post so frequently, this CTA has become a bit of a calling card. People have approached me in Sydney's CBD, saying, *"I love your stuff—I hit follow."* It's proof that when you repeatedly ask, and you've built up goodwill with your content, people respond.

This isn't just about boasting results; it proves how simple it can be to grow your audience by making the *"ask"* part of the routine. A real-life example: *The Hustle*, a business and tech email newsletter, grew to over 1.5 million subscribers by consistently providing daily value. At the bottom of every email, they had a clear, engaging CTA—*"Liked this? Share it with a friend."* That one simple, persistent ask snowballed into viral growth, turning them into one of the most popular newsletters in the business world.

You don't need a flashy voice or a perfectly crafted pitch; just use an authentic CTA that fits your style, delivered consistently. Be bold in asking for engagement, and you'll be surprised by how quickly your audience grows. The consistency of *asking* is what will eventually get you over the line.

Pro Tip #1 – Repetition is Key

Once you've nailed down your *"Follow Me"* message, save it in your notes—on your phone, laptop, wherever—and use it in every single post. That way, your tribe gets used to seeing it, and it becomes part of your brand, ensuring every post has the potential to gain new followers.

Transgressing the Law

Imagine being at a car dealership and after spending an hour convincing the salesperson you want that sleek, shiny, turbocharged car, they walk you through every feature, take you for a test drive, and you're sold. As you reach the end, the salesperson simply says, *"Well, hope you enjoyed the ride, have a good day!"*

You're left there thinking, *"Wait... aren't you going to ask me if I want to buy the car?"* Instead, you head to another dealership down the road, and that salesperson closes the deal in 10 minutes.

Not asking for the close—or in our case, the follow—is like letting a customer walk away when they're ready to buy. You did all the hard work, built the trust, delivered value. At the last second, you chickened out. You don't want your competition to ask for the follow after you've done the heavy lifting.

Close the deal: ask for the follow!

LinkedIn Judgement - Lead with Value:
The Art of Attracting Followers

Throughout history, great leaders have had the courage to ask people to follow them. Figures like Nelson Mandela, JFK, Martin Luther King Jr., and Mother Teresa each led with such conviction that their followers were naturally drawn to their cause. Their influence came not just from their requests but from their unwavering belief and the compelling nature of their missions.

On LinkedIn, asking for a follow alone won't guarantee success. Complement this request with high-quality content and a clear value proposition for your audience. By consistently producing valuable and engaging content, you'll naturally attract and grow your following. Your commitment to delivering value will ensure your audience follows you and stays engaged and invested in what you have to offer.

Closing Thoughts: From Followers to Fans, The Power of the Ask

When crafting your LinkedIn posts, remember this: **If you don't ask, you don't get.** Channel your inner Chills and boldly issue your challenge: *"Hit that follow button and join the ride!"* It's not just a call to action; it's an invitation to be part of something bigger. Think of it as building your own digital fan club, where the only rule is to keep delivering exceptional content that resonates.

Making the ask sets the stage for growth. Your audience wants to engage; they often just need a nudge. Like the *foot-in-the-door* technique demonstrated by Freedman and Fraser, a small step leads to bigger actions. Inviting them to follow creates a chain reaction of deeper connection and trust.

So, go ahead—make the ask. Be consistent, be bold, and watch as your follower count starts to soar 🚀. And remember, every great journey starts with a single step—and a single follow.

Now, go ahead and make it count!

Law #11 – The Magic of Seven Likes: Building Bonds That Matter

Only by giving are you able to receive more than you already have.
— Jim Rohn

So, you've connected with someone new. They've received a personalised message from you (Voice Message of course) inviting them for coffee and referencing your recent article or post. Now, how will you leave them feeling extra special?

It goes back to a Jim Rohn philosophy of *"Giving starts the receiving process."* A fantastic way to embody this principle is by engaging with your new connection's content. What do I mean by that? You get to add your influencer shine to them and elevate them in the feed.

What you do is pull up their recent posts from their profile page and hit that like button on their **seven** most recent posts.

What's the benefit of this approach? It serves two important purposes:

1. **Show Your Investment**: By liking their posts, you demonstrate your commitment to their growth rather than just seeking to take from the relationship. Remember: Givers Gain!
2. **Get to Know Them**: Engaging with their content allows you to understand their interests and values, giving you insight into what makes them tick.

Pro Tip #1 – Like Before You Mic

To relate on a personal level, consider liking their content before you send your voice message. This way, you can tailor your approach based on what you've learned about them. For example:

> "Hey John, lovely to connect! I noticed you're passionate about vintage cars. Let me know when you're next in the city—I know a great spot near Martin Place filled with vintage cars and memorabilia."

Do you think you're more likely to receive a positive response? Absolutely!

Observing the Law

Edward Zia, known as Mr. LinkedIn, is a marketing savant who first crossed my radar after I connected with him. I noticed 7-10 interactions on my LinkedIn feed, with him consistently liking my posts. This wasn't casual; it was a strategic engagement. Research by the *Journal of Marketing* shows that social media interactions, such as likes and comments, can significantly increase content visibility and engagement. Edward's approach exemplifies this principle.

Naturally, I was both delighted and curious, so I sent him a voice message, and we met for coffee. During our conversation, he shared how he consistently engages with others on LinkedIn, not just for visibility, but to build genuine relationships. He leverages the platform to nurture connections, creating a ripple effect of engagement. By being present in his network's feeds, he has become a central figure in many professionals' LinkedIn experiences.

Edward's engagement didn't just boost my dopamine levels; it prompted me to reciprocate the joy by sharing that positivity with my new connections and clients. According to a study by the *University of California, Irvine,* the brain releases dopamine not just from receiving likes but also from giving them. This creates a cycle of positivity and engagement that can transform professional networks.

A real-world example of this is how Gary Vaynerchuk, a prominent entrepreneur and social media influencer, built his empire. He often emphasizes the importance of engagement, stating, *"You can't just create content; you need to be a part of the community."* By actively liking, commenting, and sharing others' posts, he has fostered a loyal following that feels valued and engaged. This approach has not only expanded his reach but has also led to numerous business opportunities.

So, the key takeaway? Engagement isn't just about visibility; it's about creating connections and fostering community. By actively participating in the conversations around you, like Edward Zia and Gary Vaynerchuk, you'll not only enhance your online presence but also build meaningful relationships that can elevate your professional journey.

Pro Tip #2 – Playing the Slots

I once heard an analogy from **Nir Eyal**, author of *Hooked*, who likens checking notifications on your phone to playing slot machines (or Pokies as they're called Down Under). Just like pulling the lever at a casino, every notification brings a thrill of uncertainty and anticipation. Each time you receive a like or comment, your brain releases dopamine, creating a sense of pleasure and reward.

Research shows that variable rewards—like unpredictable notifications—are more effective at keeping us engaged than consistent rewards. This explains why social media platforms design their notifications to trigger these little bursts of happiness.

When you engage with someone's content, like their post seven times, you contribute to their joy. Consider influencers like Gary Vaynerchuk and Marie Forleo, who actively engage with their followers. This not only boosts engagement but also fosters loyalty within their communities.

So, as you scroll through your notifications, remember that each interaction is a chance to uplift others while also enhancing your visibility and connection. With every like and comment, you're not just playing the slots for yourself—you're helping to create a rewarding experience for others, building relationships that can lead to significant opportunities down the line.

Transgressing the law

When I receive connection requests with immediate links to content or offers, I can't help but roll my eyes. It's like being hit with a pitch slap—hard and fast, and not in a good way!

This spammy approach is rampant on LinkedIn, where many connections bombard you with generic messages, completely ignoring your interests or needs. It's like trying to sell sand to a desert dweller without understanding their needs. The age-old adage rings true: "Interested is interesting!"

Research supports the idea that personalized communication yields far better results than generic outreach. A study by *HubSpot* found that personalized emails have a 29% higher open rate and a 41% higher click-through rate than non-personalized ones. This highlights the importance of taking the time to understand your connections rather than launching straight into a sales pitch.

Some might argue that liking someone's content seven times could seem spammy. However, it's a rare approach, making it a delightful surprise—a hidden gem in a sea of mediocrity! Think of it as the *"purple cow"* concept from Seth Godin's book. In a field full of plain old cows, the purple one stands out—different, unique, and unforgettable.

Gary Vaynerchuk emphasizes that genuine relationships outweigh hard selling. He engages with his audience meaningfully before introducing his services, cultivating a community eager to support him.

So, embrace your inner purple cow, dear readers! Be that vibrant, standout presence for your new connections and clients. ne real-life example comes to mind: I connected with a marketing professional who consistently engaged with my posts. When he eventually reached out for coffee (and an offer), I was excited to hear from him because he had already established rapport. I assure you, you'll never run short of exciting opportunities when you choose authenticity over the hard sell. Be sure to connect with **Chris Melotti** from **Melotti Media**; great guy!

Closing Thoughts: The Ripple of Generosity

As we wrap up Law #11, remember: being a giver enriches your connections and opens doors to new opportunities. Embrace generosity in networking, and become a vibrant presence in a sea of sameness.

So, the next time you connect with someone, take a moment to spread a little joy—like their posts, share their insights, and watch the magic unfold. You'll not only brighten their day, but you'll also cultivate relationships that are genuinely rewarding.

After all, networking is not just about collecting contacts; it's about creating connections that matter. Be that purple cow, stand out in your field, and let your unique light shine! Now go forth and make those connections—one like at a time. Who knows what incredible opportunities await you just around the corner?

Law #12 – The Reciprocity Effect: Building Relationships Through Recommendations

> *Everyone has an invisible sign hanging from their neck saying, 'Make me feel important' Never forget this message when working with people.*
> — *Mary Kay Ash*

When I first embarked on my LinkedIn journey, I was struck by one gentleman who had amassed an impressive number of recommendations. Curious, I asked him over coffee, "You must ask quite a lot of people for those?" He replied, *"Quite the opposite. I give, then I get back."* His mantra was simple yet powerful: *"Givers gain!"*

Givers gain goes hand in hand with the next law we'll cover.

The Law of Reciprocity

The Law of Reciprocity reveals that humans are instinctively driven to return favours. This principle is not just a social nicety; it's a powerful psychological mechanism. Research by Robert Cialdini in *Influence: The Psychology of Persuasion* shows that when we receive kindness, we feel a social obligation to reciprocate.

Real-World Examples:

1. **Networking Dynamics**: Recently, at a legal conference, I connected with a marketing professional who took the time to share insights from her latest campaign. After our conversation, I felt compelled to refer her services to a colleague looking for

similar expertise. This simple act of sharing knowledge fostered mutual support.
2. **Influencer Engagement**: Gary Vaynerchuk embodies this principle through his online presence. He actively engages with his audience by responding to comments and offering value before pitching his services. As a result, his followers often feel inclined to support his initiatives, such as buying his books or attending his events.

According to a study published in the *Journal of Experimental Social Psychology*, individuals who engage in acts of kindness are more likely to receive help in return. This reinforces the idea that fostering relationships through generosity leads to greater social capital.

By embracing the *Law of Reciprocity*, you can enhance your networking strategy on LinkedIn. Whether through sharing insights, liking posts, or offering support, these actions will encourage others to reciprocate, ultimately enriching your professional relationships and expanding your opportunities.

Observing the Law

Recently, my wife and I visited Tokyo Disneyland. If you've ever been to Japan, you know two things: the people are incredibly kind and caring, and it's always bustling, especially at Disney.

The reason I'm telling you this is because I never bring a selfie stick with me because I know I can lean on the law of reciprocity, the kindness of the people and the fact that it's always so busy to my advantage.

Case in point! When I wanted a photo of the castle lit up at night with my wife and Benji, instead of asking, *"Can you take my photo?"* I approached a couple struggling to take a selfie and offered, *"Would you like me to take your photo?"* Their faces lit up, and they enthusiastically replied, *"Yes, that would be great!"*

What happens next is a phenomenon Jim Rohn aptly described: "Giving starts the receiving process." After thanking me, they usually ask, *"Can I take one of you?"* Of course! That's exactly what I wanted in the first place.

If the law were applied to the realm of LinkedIn and the recommendations feature, when you connect with a friend, client, or colleague, make it a point to recommend them after your interaction—whether it's a coffee chat or a phone call. It takes just 1-2 minutes to write a meaningful recommendation that highlights their strengths.

It doesn't have to be *"War & Peace."* Instead, keep it succinct but impactful, highlighting their strengths and why you enjoy working with them. For example:

"Michelle is a powerhouse in her conveyancing field, consistently going above and beyond for her clients. You'd do well to connect with her"

Here's why you benefit:

1. The person is touched by your proactive generosity.
2. You may receive a recommendation in return (and you usually will).
3. Your name appears on their LinkedIn profile, which may catch the eye of fellow connections.

If you consistently recommend every new client and connection you meet, you'll likely see your own recommendations soar. In fact, you may end up giving more than you receive, but that gesture will always be remembered.

Business owners, sole practitioners, and entrepreneurs often appreciate recommendations even more because you're not just investing in them—you're investing in their business. They'll know you genuinely care about their growth and success and want to see them do well, not just about making a sale.

If you want *Google Reviews* instead, follow this same rubric; it's the same logic.

Pro Tip #1: How to Recommend Tribe Members on LinkedIn—Even If You've Never Worked Together!

In the world of LinkedIn, tribe means everything—whether they're your clients, partners, or trusted collaborators. But what happens when you want to give a glowing recommendation for someone who's been in your corner, yet you've never shared the same company? Easy. LinkedIn's *"Worked with you but at different companies"* option is the tool you need.

Why It's Gold for Your Tribe: This isn't a loophole; it's designed for today's connected professionals who work across industries. Whether you collaborated on a client project, connected through masterminds, or supported each other through shared business goals, this feature allows you to celebrate your tribe members without needing that shared employment history.

How to Write a Standout Recommendation for Your Client or Collaborator:

1. **Lead with your shared wins**: Focus on the challenges you faced together. Did they push the project forward? Deliver results? Capture the essence of your teamwork to show the depth of your collaboration.
2. **Share the impact**: Don't just say they're *"great to work with"*— explain how they helped you (or your business) crush goals. Clients and partners appreciate seeing the value they added to your professional journey.
3. **Keep it real**: Make it personal. Mention specific moments where their skills or approach made a difference for you or your tribe. Authenticity always cuts through the noise on LinkedIn.

Research backs this up: LinkedIn recommendations make profiles 10x more likely to be viewed and boost credibility—critical for growing your network and influence. When you recommend a tribe member with the *"Worked with you but at different companies"* option, you're enhancing both their profile and yours. It's a win-win for everyone in the tribe.

So, go ahead and give your clients, partners, or fellow tribe members the recognition they deserve!

LinkedIn Judgement - Givers Gain: The Ripple Effect of Kindness

There's a common misconception, that you must know a person or have used their services to recommend them. It's simply not true—just like leaving Google reviews. It's a mistake to think you can't spread the love with a five-star review. Believe me, they'll appreciate your support.

I remember the early days of our company, LHL, when we had no Google reviews. One of my LinkedIn influencer friends left me a glowing review after we had coffee, and it gave me such a buzz. I felt incredibly grateful, and I made it a point to pay it forward. Fast forward to today, and we have 525 Google reviews—all starting with that one kind gesture. I've always taken that lesson and done my best to pay it forward even today.

Remember: givers gain.

Transgressing the Law

I always chuckle when I receive DMs from long-term connections asking me for recommendations. Little do they realize the immense power of the Law of Reciprocity at play here. When we freely give our time and support, we naturally prompt others to reciprocate. I often remind them that by offering multiple recommendations, they create a network of goodwill that others will be eager to repay, often much quicker than they might expect.

The Pitfall of Asking

Asking for recommendations can resemble that awkward moment when you call someone and inquire, *"Am I getting you at a good time?"* When they respond with a *"yes,"* it places them in a subconscious bind where they feel obligated to help, even if it's not the right moment for them. A more generous approach works better: instead of asking them to accommodate me, I frame it as *"Am I getting you at a bad time?"* This subtle shift acknowledges their current state, allowing for a more genuine conversation free from the weight of obligation.

Chris Voss on Communication

As Chris Voss, the former FBI negotiator and author of *Never Split the Difference*, astutely points out, *"Yes actually does more harm than good."* This observation reflects the psychological nuances behind negotiation and human interaction. When we press for agreement, we can inadvertently foster resentment or reluctance rather than collaboration.

Research in psychology backs this up. Studies show that individuals often respond better to requests framed in a way that emphasizes their autonomy rather than placing them in a situation where they feel they owe a favour. This perspective encourages open communication, where both parties feel valued and respected.

Giving Over Taking

The core of the *Law of Reciprocity* lies in giving without the expectation of receiving immediately in return. By focusing on creating value for others—writing thoughtful recommendations, sharing insights, or connecting individuals in your network—you cultivate a fertile environment where reciprocity flourishes naturally.

A poignant example from my experience involved a colleague who routinely endorsed others on LinkedIn. Over time, he built a network of strong relationships. When he needed support for a job transition, the responses he received were overwhelmingly positive and enthusiastic. His generosity planted seeds of goodwill that bloomed into tangible opportunities.

Closing Thoughts: Sowing Seeds of Generosity

So, as you venture forth in your networking journey, remember the golden rule: the more you give, the more you receive. Think of each recommendation you write as planting a seed; with time and care, those seeds will blossom into thriving connections and opportunities.

Embrace the *Law of Reciprocity*! Be that person who lights up a room (or a LinkedIn feed) with kindness and generosity. Who knows? The next time you need a favour or a recommendation, you might just find a cascade of support waiting for you, all thanks to the goodwill you've sown.

Now, go out there, spread some positivity, and let your connections know just how incredible they are. After all, in the grand symphony of networking, the more you play your part, the more harmonious the melody becomes. Happy networking!

Law #13 – Love yourself first ♡

Love yourself first and everything falls into place. You really have to love yourself to get anything done in this world.
— Lucille Ball

We're often taught in the Western Culture, especially in Australia that self-love, or tooting your own horn, is not something that should be supported. Liking your own content is often viewed as negative advertising, as everyone can see you're doing it. What's more, if you're found out, people will make it known, call you out, and cut you down to size—tall poppy syndrome. Nothing could be further from the truth. When was the last time you looked in detail, at who actually liked another person's post? I'd wager you just looked at the number of likes. But let's set the record straight: loving yourself should be worn as a badge of honour, not a source of shame.

When you scroll through LinkedIn, do you ever pay attention to who liked someone else's post? Most likely, you only glance at the number of likes, yet this is critical. Self-endorsement significantly influences how others perceive your content. Imagine seeing a post with zero likes or comments. How likely are you to be the first person to engage? My guess is you won't be, and that's a common reaction. Human beings tend to follow the crowd, as Derek Sivers wisely points out: it's not the great leaders who are brave, but the first follower who truly takes the risk.

In my seven years of heavy LinkedIn use, I've learned that the algorithm doesn't differentiate between a like from you and anyone else.

As Zig Ziglar famously said, *"You can have everything in life you want, if you will just help enough other people get what they want."* By liking your own content, you kickstart engagement, signalling to the algorithm that someone appreciates what you've shared. And thus, moving things further in your favour.

Observing the Law

As mentioned previously, a common misconception is that people will perceive you as egotistical if you like your own content. This assumption is erroneous on all counts! Research indicates that individuals who engage positively with their own content often find greater engagement and visibility overall. According to a 2021 study published in the *Journal of Social Media in Society*, self-liking can signal confidence and encourage others to engage with the content, thereby increasing its reach.

My turning point in my LinkedIn journey occurred during a conversation with my good friend and fellow LinkedIn influencer, Dino Pacella. At the time, I was working at Macquarie, and he was at Suncorp. One day, over coffee, I confided in Dino that I was afraid people would think less of me for liking my own posts. He simply smiled and said, "Look, Cullen, here's something I just posted. And I've just liked it too. It only came up with the photo, not the actual name."

That moment changed everything for me. It made me realize that liking your own content isn't about self-importance; it's about supporting your message and encouraging others to engage. Studies have shown that social media algorithms favour posts that receive immediate interaction, including likes, which can significantly increase visibility and engagement.

For instance, a 2021 study by Buffer found that posts that receive likes shortly after being published are more likely to be shown to a broader audience. By liking your own content, you can kickstart this process, increasing the likelihood that your network will see and interact with your posts.

Influencer Examples

Numerous successful influencers incorporate this practice as part of their social media strategy. For example:

1. **Brene Brown**: As a researcher and author, Brene often likes her own content to drive engagement and visibility. Her posts are characterized by vulnerability and authenticity, and her self-endorsement serves to amplify her messages about courage and connection.
2. **Gary Vaynerchuk**: As a prolific entrepreneur and social media influencer, Gary often likes his own posts and engages with his content across platforms. He emphasizes the importance of being your own advocate, stating, "If you don't believe in yourself, no one else will."
3. **Simon Sinek**: Known for his insights on leadership and motivation, Simon frequently engages with his posts, liking and sharing his own content to highlight key messages. This practice not only reinforces his ideas but also encourages others to participate in the conversation.

Since then, I've embraced self-love on my posts without hesitation. I've found that my willingness to engage with my content has led to increased interaction from my connections. By modelling this behaviour, I encourage others to feel more comfortable doing the same, creating a positive feedback loop of support and engagement within my network.

Self-endorsement isn't just an act of confidence; it's a strategic move in the world of LinkedIn. As we continue to share our insights and experiences, let's not shy away from embracing our own content. By doing so, we're not just amplifying our voices; we're paving the way for deeper connections and engagement across our networks.

Pro Tip #1 – Paint with All the Colours of the Wind

Colours matter, even to someone as colourblind as me—true story. LinkedIn and Facebook allow you to express reactions beyond the simple *"like"*—such as Happy, Sad, or Curious. These reactions not only add variety but also create visual appeal, making your posts more engaging. So go ahead, sprinkle some colourful love on your posts and watch the engagement bloom.

Transgressing the Law

Failing to like your own content can lead to low engagement. I often see our company page's posts languishing in *"non-liked limbo,"* and it drives me crazy! All it takes is a cheeky like from the mothership (and yours truly) to spark engagement.

Classically trained marketers often advise against liking your own content for the same tired reasons: it's perceived as self-serving, or it could damage your credibility. Here's the reality: Research indicates that engagement rates significantly drop when posts don't receive immediate interaction. According to a study from *Hootsuite*, posts that garner likes within the first hour of being published are more likely to be promoted by algorithms, meaning they'll reach a broader audience.

Do I listen to the naysayers? No. I appreciate their opinions but choose to prioritize my goals. While it may not be socially acceptable, I care more about the algorithm and reaching as many eyes in my tribe as possible. My objective is to have my content impact the widest audience, and that means I'm going to like my posts unapologetically.

Consider the example of **Neil Patel**, a digital marketing expert who we've spoken about before. He often engages with his own content on social media, even while sharing marketing insights on how to maximize engagement. By liking his posts, he reinforces their importance and encourages others to join the conversation. As a result, his content consistently garners high engagement rates, demonstrating that self-liking can indeed create a ripple effect.

Interestingly, many marketers create polished videos about engagement but often fail to follow their own advice. Guess how many likes their content usually gets? Very few, if any. This discrepancy highlights the disconnect between theory and practice in the marketing world.

In an age where social media algorithms dictate visibility, liking your own posts isn't just a personal endorsement; it's a strategic move. When we like our content, we send a signal to the algorithm that our posts are worth engaging with, prompting others to do the same.

Final Thoughts

In essence, transgressing the social norms around self-liking is not just acceptable—it's necessary for effective engagement. Embrace the practice, and you might find that your content gains the traction it deserves, reaching the audience you aim to impact.

Pro Tip #2 – Don't Listen to "The Experts"

Every insight in this book comes from years of real-world experience building my online presence and business. If I had listened to the self-proclaimed marketing *"experts,"* I'd be posting only once or twice a week—if that! Many of these advisors haven't run a business, and when you look at their own following and engagement, it often leaves much to be desired.

Remember this piece of wisdom my mentor shared early in my career: "Don't let someone else's opinion of you become your reality. What people think of you is none of your business."

Closing Thoughts: Be Your Own Biggest Fan

So, dear reader, it's time to unleash your inner cheerleader! Remember, loving yourself isn't just a catchy slogan; it's a strategic move on the LinkedIn chessboard. The next time you craft a post, don't hold back—give yourself that well-deserved like! Dance like no one's watching, post like no one's judging, and above all, love yourself like you're the superstar of your own show.

Think of it this way: *if you don't celebrate your own achievements, who will?* So go ahead, be your biggest fan! Embrace the vibrant spectrum of reactions on your content and watch the engagement soar. The algorithm is your friend, and so is self-love. Now, get out there and sprinkle that love everywhere!

Because at the end of the day, the best investment you can make is in yourself—and trust me, that's a return that never disappoints!

P.S. If in doubt, ask this question. What would Taylor do? I think we know ♡

💎 *"Be yourself, there is no one better" #TaylorSwift Original 'Swifties' before it was even mainstream or cool to be one* 😊

Law #14 – Engage or Fade: The Impact of Commenting on LinkedIn

The art of commenting is not to speak louder than the crowd, but to add something of value that others have overlooked.
— *Anonymous*

Given the last chapter, you probably see where I'm going with this. Yes, you're right, dear reader. Liking your content is essential, but commenting on it is the real game changer.

The question is *"Why?"*

The answer is three-fold:

1. **Algorithm Boost:** It signals to the algorithm that at least one person has already commented on your content.
2. **Active Engagement:** It encourages others to actively engage and respond to your posts.
3. **Billboard Effect:** Your posts become tiny billboards, capturing attention even if they aren't explicitly promotional. I can't tell you how many leads, connections, and business inquiries we've received from this simple practice!

Observing the Law

Engagement is the lifeblood of LinkedIn, and commenting on your own posts is a powerful way to enhance visibility and foster connection. When you comment on your content, you signal to algorithms that your post is worth promoting, increasing its reach.

Research from *Hootsuite* shows that posts with early engagement, including comments, are favoured by algorithms, leading to broader visibility. Additionally, content with high comment volume is perceived as more valuable. Your active participation enriches the conversation, encouraging others to join in.

Consider influencers like, **Gary Vaynerchuk** who frequently engages with comments on his posts to stimulate discussions, or **Brené Brown**, who uses her platform to encourage dialogue on vulnerability. **Simon Sinek** and **Neil Patel** also exemplify the power of engagement, responding to their audiences and creating a sense of community.

In summary, commenting on your own content is more than just a tactic; it's a commitment to building relationships and elevating discussions. Each comment is an opportunity to deepen connections and enrich the conversation—so embrace it!

Now that we've established that commenting is crucial, what should you write? Personally, Based on experience, two types of comments consistently work well.

The first comment can be a question or a statement:

> 1) *"Love to know your thoughts all?"*
>   *"I voted no because..."*
>   *"Have a great Thursday friends"*

The second comment serves as my Call to Action (CTA) embedded in every post:

> 2)

#LegalProfessionals, you deserve more! Borrow with just a 10% deposit—no LMI!

✅ Platinum Broker Certified - Top 1% - Preferential Rates, Turnaround Times & Policies

✅ Rates from 5.59% Occ

◆ 5.79% Investment - P&I

◆ 5.89% Investment - Interest Only

✅ Exclusive legal credit policy: 10% Deposit waived, LMI

✅ Up to $3,000 Refinance Cash Back

✅ $500 Rebate for eligible Law Society Members

✅ Finance solutions for salaried & equity Partners

✅ Barristers: 100% Unsecured Chambers

✅ Exclusive terms to access Australia's leading Private Banks

Leverage your profession ⚖️ conserve time ⏱️ save thousands

🕸️ *Subject to individual lending position*

Weigh your options while WFH 🏠

⚖️ https://www.legalhomeloans.com.au/contact-us

#Lawyers #HomeLoans

As soon as I post, I follow up with these two comments. I also add some context-sensitive text to the second comment to avoid being flagged as spam. This method triggers the algorithm and boosts engagement. I even comment on my own comments—maybe it's an OCD thing! 😁

The more engagement, the better.

LinkedIn Judgement - Add Value, Not Templates

When commenting on others' posts, which I highly recommend spend 2-3 minutes per day, doing, it pays dividends to tailor it to the person posting. The whole reason for a comment is to add a noteworthy and conversation striking point, question or comment that adds value to that person and the community. You may see some folks on LinkedIn using pictures of *"That's Great"* or *"Awesome share"* as posts. Which I know this method gets views, I see it also as a tacky way of getting views for views' sake. Like reposting clickbait videos. You know the ones, of machinery, or cleaning a pool filter that looks awesome or a TikTok like viral video.

Pro Tip #1 – Share the Love

As noted earlier, as important as it is to comment on your own posts to get it flowing, make it a daily habit to comment on others straight after as well. I'm not advocating you get lost in "the death scroll" nor am I saying that carving out time in the morning or afternoon to get this done is wise either. It's a quick win, however, of praising 1-3 others for every post you do:

> *"Great poll you have there"*
> *"Enthralling, what do you think now?"*
> *"Never saw it that way – You've opened my eyes Dillon"*

Pro Tip #2 – Get into the Habit

If you regularly comment on others' posts, the algorithm will prioritize those you engage with in your feed, and vice versa. This is a highly effective way of building rapport. You'll find that those you comment on may start engaging with you in return (don't be surprised). It's the Law of Reciprocity at work!

Another positive by-product? You'll be seen by that person's network repeatedly, and they may start engaging with your posts too!

Take Your Commenting Game to 11!

Pro Tip #3 – Two Ways to Have the Tallest Building

Always remember there are two ways to have the tallest building in town. You can either focus on building your own or tear others down. Unfortunately, many opt for the latter. Instead, love yourself and focus on elevating both yourself and others; the rewards will come back to you ten-fold.

Closing Thoughts: The Art of Commenting

As we wrap up this exploration of the commenting game on LinkedIn, remember this: every time you engage, you're not just adding to the conversation—you're building your own network, elevating your presence, and transforming your posts into dynamic platforms of influence.

Think of your comments as the seasoning in a gourmet dish; the right blend can turn a simple meal into a culinary masterpiece! So, sprinkle a little thoughtfulness, dash in some curiosity, and watch as your interactions flourish.

Next time you hesitate to comment—whether it's on your own post or someone else's—channel your inner Socrates who very aptly said *"The way to gain a good reputation is to endeavour to be what you desire to appear."* You're in this game to shine, to connect, and to grow, so why not make every word count?

Now, go forth and sprinkle those comments like confetti! Engage, uplift, and watch the magic unfold. And who knows? That little comment could be the spark that ignites a conversation leading to your next big opportunity.

So, as you dive into the next chapter, carry this mantra with you: **Every comment is a chance. Make it count!**

Law #15 - The Gift of Connection: Leverage Birthdays to Deepen Bonds

> Count your age by friends, not years. Count your life, by smiles, not tears
> — John Lennon.

To all the LinkedIn purists out there insisting that LinkedIn isn't Facebook, I pose this question: Why on earth would LinkedIn offer a feature to wish someone *"Happy Birthday"?*

Because, dear reader, business is personal. When it comes to celebrating birthdays, most great companies and teams go all out! At Legal Home Loans, we make birthdays special with cake, flowers, and presents. It only makes sense to extend that same energy into our professional networks.

LinkedIn has recently revamped its birthday feature, allowing you to see all your connections celebrating on a given day, including those belated birthdays you may have missed. When you click on a connection's name, their actual birthday appears, along with a default message you can easily send. I always advise avoiding default messages at all costs.

Many others will opt to send the default message and if you choose to do the same, yours will be lost in the sea of mediocrity and stock messages. It would be a shame to be clumped with all that! It's not just about messaging for the sake of it—it's about making the recipient feel valued.

Get creative! My go-to is straightforward but thoughtful. You might want to comment on something personal, like a recent post or gift:

"Hey Megan,

Happy Belated Birthday for yesterday. The balloons in the office looked fantastic. Hope you had a fantastic day and were made to feel special. Coffee soon!"

It may take just a few extra seconds, but the personal touch will leave a lasting impression. As Jim Rohn wisely said, *"Always do what is easy, and life will be hard. Do what is hard, and life will be easy."*

LinkedIn Judgement – Me, the Centre of the Universe

Human beings have a special feeling about one's own birthday. Apart from their name which is also very special but can be changed, it is the one thing they own that is immutable and unchangeable. It was the day you came into this world. So, anything or anyone that altruistically celebrates that will naturally endear that person towards you. People are naturally drawn to those who recognize their special day. Taking the time to send a personal message helps you stand out, reinforcing the connection in a meaningful way. Because you took the time out of your busy day. You may not get immediate business (and I must caution that should <u>never</u> be the reason or goal) people remember those who take time to reach out personally and you will make a positive mark. I've had clients reach out weeks later, saying, "We need to catch up for coffee," all because I took the time to recognize their special day.

Observing The Law

One of the best Voicemails I've ever received, on or off LinkedIn, was from my dear friend Emmanuel Mazzanti, Conscious Talent

Development Leader at EY Nordics - https://www.linkedin.com/in/emazzanti/

Not only is Emmanuel a walking, talking example of everything in this book, he's also an avid reader and fellow runner. He's a member of the small club that can run Sub-3 Hours in the Marathon and he shared a beautiful post of his achievement; he recently achieved this at age 50 I might add. One of the best messages I received was by this great man on 23rd August 2020. In his message Emmanuel touched on everything I love: quotes, books, running, and a bit of his own life. He packed it all into a charming 1-minute and 23-second message:

> *"Hey Cullen, I didn't know it was your Birthday.*
> *As the Vikings say "Heil og sæl" (Happy Birthday) so have a good one. Happy Birthday. We're here with a friend from Canada and just about to go for a run and a swim, and we'll be thinking about you tonight maybe over one glass before we start again tonight. Very active weekend. There is also like a Tony Robbins event sort of, so we might even walk on coals, but we're not invited. But we'll see. But this is about you, have the best day, have a good one. Happy Birthday again. Hej Da!"*

What did Emmanuel do right here? He didn't just rely on the old trope "Happy Birthday"; period; end of story. He made it more spontaneous; he personalized it with cultural references, personal updates, and even our shared interests. I love the *"As the Vikings say..."* He then said he's running and swimming (Two things I absolutely love) and that he'll be raising a glass to me over dinner. He then mentioned Tony Robbins, some of who's teachings we avidly follow (which are, in fact, philosophies passed down from the late great Jim Rohn). It's still one of the best messages I've ever received kudos to Emmanuel!

Transgressing the Law

When it comes to birthdays on LinkedIn, the stakes are higher than you might think. Ignoring someone's birthday or sending a generic message is a missed chance to engage meaningfully. In the fast-paced world of social media, every interaction counts, and failing to acknowledge someone's birthday can feel like a slight.

The Cost of Inaction

As Grant Cardone says, *"Doing nothing has no ROI!"* This applies not just in business but in relationship-building as well. A birthday greeting is more than a simple acknowledgment; it's an opportunity to solidify your presence in someone's mind. It can transform a fleeting connection into a lasting relationship, opening the door to future collaborations or opportunities.

The Power of Personalization

A personalized birthday message makes you memorable. Instead of a standard greeting, consider crafting a personalized message that reflects your relationship with the individual. For instance, if you're aware of a particular achievement or milestone they've reached, mention it in your greeting. This level of attentiveness not only shows that you care but also reinforces the bond you share.

Ryan Holiday, author of *The Obstacle is the Way,* emphasizes the importance of genuine connection in a digital age filled with noise. He argues that people crave authenticity and appreciation. Taking the time to acknowledge someone's birthday strengthens relationships and can lead to long-term opportunities.

Research on Connection and Engagement

Studies indicate that personalized communication can significantly enhance relationship-building efforts. According to a survey by the *Harvard Business Review*, 70% of respondents preferred receiving personalized messages over generic ones. Additionally, research from the *University of California, Berkeley*, highlights that personal connections—whether in business or personal realms—are vital for fostering trust and collaboration.

By taking the time to recognize birthdays, you not only elevate your presence on LinkedIn but also position yourself as a person of value within your network. This small gesture can lead to larger returns down the line, as people are more likely to remember those who celebrate them, whether through words or actions.

Practical Example

Consider the case of a LinkedIn influencer who took it a step further. Instead of sending a generic birthday wish, they organized a virtual birthday gathering for a colleague. This initiative brought together multiple connections, sparking conversations that led to potential collaborations. The influencer didn't just celebrate a birthday; they cultivated a community.

Transgressing the law of acknowledging birthdays can lead to missed opportunities for connection and collaboration. As you navigate your LinkedIn interactions, remember: every birthday is a chance to strengthen relationships, and doing nothing is not an option. Embrace the opportunity to make someone's day and watch as your network flourishes in response.

Top Tip #1 – Bird by Bird, Day by Day

The idea of reaching out to your entire network every day for 365 days can feel overwhelming. Approaching it like that is a sure way to get stuck. Just like writing, which can become a daunting task if tackled all at once, the key is to break it down into manageable steps. As Anne Lamott beautifully illustrates in her book *Bird by Bird*, her father gave her brother this advice when he was overwhelmed by a school project on birds: "Just take it bird by bird." One small, intentional step at a time.

So, day by day is my advice to you. Dedicate 10-15 minutes each morning to connect with your network. Over the course of a year, those small efforts add up—5,475 minutes, or 92 hours—creating countless opportunities for meaningful engagement that you might have otherwise missed.

Closing Thoughts: Make Every Birthday Count & Elevate Your Connections

So, the next time you see a birthday notification pop up on LinkedIn, don't let it slide or send the usual canned message. Instead, seize the opportunity to make someone's day memorable. Inject a little personality, make it heartfelt, and be creative. Whether it's a clever message, a playful emoji, or a quick voice note that speaks to your relationship—whatever you do, make it count.

Remember, the real magic isn't in just saying "Happy Birthday." It's in making the person feel seen, valued, and celebrated. That extra effort may just be the difference between a forgettable interaction and a lasting connection. And who knows? You may find yourself grabbing a coffee, closing a deal, or simply forging a stronger bond.

After all, business is personal—and nothing's more personal than a birthday.

Law #16 – Elevate and Celebrate: The Art of Acknowledging Achievements

Without promotion, something terrible happens.
— *P.T. Barnum*

In *Law #6 – Celebrate Good Times, Come On*! we touched on **Maslow's Hierarchy of Needs**, specifically the need for *Esteem and Significance*. Recognition in one's role is essential for human beings on their path to self-actualization. One of my guests on ***LawLive*** **#36**, Charles Lowenhaupt of Lowenhaupt Global Advisors, emphasized the importance of being the best you can be while earning respect from your friends and family. Without this recognition, it can foster a sense of *economic insecurity*.

When it comes to promotions, LinkedIn provides an exceptional platform for professionals to gain recognition in two important ways:

1. To share their career advancement.
2. To receive real-time feedback from their peers.

In the legal world, where I spend my time, career progression is not just common—it's expected One of the most esteemed goals in law firms is achieving the rank of Partner, which can take 15-20 years of dedicated work. When someone achieves this, it's an exceptional accomplishment that demands recognition.

Let's call it what it is: a *humble brag* or, as we say in Australia, *blowing your own trumpet*. LinkedIn has become the accepted platform for this kind of self-praise. It is a way of saying, I'm so honoured to announce

I've made Partner/Been Promoted/Got the dream job. And because it's an unofficial social contract and accepted form of self-praise and admiration, these promotion announcements often generate 100-150 comments because, typically, they're one of the few personal posts people make.

Going back to the power dynamics of the old aristocratic court we talked about in *Law #6 – Celebrate Good Times, Come On*! It's most important that you acknowledge other people's rise in a genuine, authentic way and make it about them.

Two Steps to Do It Right:

1. Congratulate publicly on the post (Like and Comment)
2. Send a personal message with (You guessed it) a VM

1. Congratulate Publicly

This is a two-fold win for both you and the promotee. One, the promotee feels great because they've been acknowledged, and you've taken the time out of your day to engage on their post. Second, if you've properly set your LinkedIn title, it serves as a mini billboard, prompting others to take notice of you too.

For example, a colleague might think, *"Hey, I didn't know Cullen knew Jack; I'll connect with him"* or *"I need a lawyer-friendly mortgage broker—I'll reach out to Cullen."* Either way, you both benefit.

Pro Tip #1 – Recognition Reminders

Do it *now* and do it *often*. LinkedIn makes it easier by gathering all celebrations (birthdays, promotions, anniversaries) in one place under the *My Network* section; more recently bundled under **Catch Up**. This feature ensures you never miss a chance to engage. -

- Birthdays
- Promotions
- Anniversaries

So, you have no excuse. Each day, congratulate and engage on each day's new promotee, anniversary recipient or someone's birthday. You'll be surprised how many people get back with their deepest thanks.

Observing The Law

What does a good public message look like? First off, *ditch the stock images* and the auto-generated text LinkedIn provides. Your goal is to *stand out*, not blend in. I like to use verbiage that's unique, avoiding the clichés everyone else is posting. Adding eye-catching emojis can also give your message a fun, vibrant feel, making it memorable. After all, emojis are meant to add personality to your posts—so don't shy away from them.

Here's an example of my go-to promotion message:

> *"Kudos on the promotion, @Jenny! Wishing you luck and all green lights in your new role!"* 🍀

Using the "@" symbol to tag the person is crucial—it links you and the person in the feed, increasing visibility. *The point is to be seen.* Visibility is everything: see and be seen!

LinkedIn Judgement: Surround Yourself With People Who Want You to Elevator

A story that taught me a key lesson about LinkedIn came early on in my journey. Domenic Nesci, my good friend, property juggernaut, and author, posted about a new job, and I lazily commented, *"Well done Dom."* It was generic, unengaging, and a complete missed opportunity.

Not even five minutes later, I got a voice message from Domenic: *"Thanks for the congratulations, mate, but make sure you're properly tagging me, otherwise no one sees that you shouted me out. And if they don't, what's the point?"*

That stuck with me. The value of *thoughtful engagement* on LinkedIn can't be understated. It's not just about congratulating—it's about ensuring you're contributing meaningfully and helping the other person shine. Surround yourself with people who will call you out, push you to grow, and encourage you to become better—just like Dom did for me.

2. DM using VM

The VM saves the day again! Many people stop after the public congratulations, but that's what makes this strategy *ordinary*. Why be ordinary when you can stand out?

Sending a thoughtful, personalized VM isn't a chore—it's a chance to foster a deeper connection.

Here's an example of what that might sound like:

> *"Hey Kim,*
> *Kudos for making Partner, well-deserved. Wishing you luck and all green lights. Coffee on me when you're next in the CBD because I'm a big believer in taking the online offline. Let me know if this week or next works?"*

This approach sets the stage for coffee meetings, virtual or otherwise, and creates meaningful interactions beyond the screen. Watch the number take off ☕🚀

Pro Tip 2 – Key Insights - Keep an Eye on the Feed!

As good as LinkedIn is in keeping track of milestones, there's many it doesn't that people shout out in the feed such as graduations, baby births, new contract etc. Be sure you're on the lookout for these too daily and then follow steps 1 & 2 and you'll get impromptu coffee meetings out of congratulating someone on bringing their dog to the office. The best meetings come from these kinds of interactions.

If you use the rule of engaging on 5-7 posts after you post one of your own pieces of content, you'll be in good stead!

Pro Tip 3 – Take the Online, Offline

You saw my mantra *"taking the online offline"* and I stand by it. I'm a big believer in taking online connections into the real world. If you're sending a congratulatory message, why not offer to meet up for coffee? Of course, be professional and clear—it's not a date! The point is to make the connection feel more tangible and valuable.

Pro Tip 4 – Happy Anniversary

Here's my messages for when connections hit 1, 3, 10-year milestones at their work or job. Again, VM is perfect for wishing someone kudos for hitting X number of years in the role:

> *"Hey Jimmy,*
> *Kudos on 50 years. What a stellar achievement. Looking forward to coffee next time you're in your 51st year"*

Playful and engaging.

Transgressing the Law

Don't be generic!

Avoid lazy, generic images like *"Congrats," "Kudos,"* or *"You're awesome."* These are uninspired and don't reflect your personal brand. You're better than that—be unique, be engaging, and be memorable.

A real-world example of this transgression comes from one of my own early LinkedIn blunders. A colleague of mine, Sarah, had just been promoted to a senior associate at a prestigious Top Tier law firm. Everyone was congratulating her, and I thought I'd join in, so I commented: *"Congrats, Sarah! Well deserved!"* Simple, right?

What I didn't realize was that **ten other people** had posted almost the exact same thing—*"Congrats," "Well deserved,"* or *"You're awesome!"* My comment blended in with the noise, doing absolutely nothing to stand out. Worse, it didn't reflect any real connection or effort on my part.

Later that week, Sarah messaged me saying, *"Thanks for the comment! It meant a lot that you took the time."* But deep down, I knew I hadn't really taken the time. It was a throwaway, generic response. That moment was a missed opportunity to deepen our connection.

From that moment, I resolved to write personalized, thoughtful congratulations—ones that actually added value and reflected my own voice. It's not about saying something just to say it; it's about leaving a *memorable* impression. You can think of it like a crowded room where everyone is shouting the same thing—how are you going to stand out?

Taking the time to recognize someone's promotion in a thoughtful way is a small gesture that can lead to meaningful connections. The more genuine your congratulations, the more likely it is that you'll turn LinkedIn interactions into real-world relationships—where the true magic happens.

Closing Thoughts: Cheers to Unforgettable Connections

Let's wrap this up with a little twist.

Think of LinkedIn like a cocktail party. You're not going to just nod at someone from across the room and say, *"Congrats."* That's awkward.

You walk over, shake their hand, and offer a genuine toast, right? The goal is to engage, connect, and leave them with something to remember. That's why you *never* want to be the person who just clinks their glass and walks away. You're better than that.

Instead of the generic thumbs-up in a sea of *"Kudos"* or *"Well done,"* be the person who brings the unexpected—a dash of wit, a sprinkle of personality, and, of course, a genuine touch. Don't just congratulate; leave them thinking, *Wow, that was different.*

Because remember, at the end of the day, it's not about the number of likes or comments you rack up—it's about how you *show up*. By mastering the art of genuine recognition, you can set yourself apart and foster meaningful professional relationships. Make each interaction count. Now go ahead, drop that standout comment or send that memorable voice message. And don't forget, the online world is just the warm-up. Take it offline, grab that coffee, and turn those digital connections into real-world relationships.

Now, go be unforgettable.

Law #17 – Video Killed the Article Star:
Why Video Wins

*If you can do something great in 60 seconds,
you can do anything really.*
— Joanne Froggatt

No, it's not a Buggles song (but I do like that tune) and there's a reason why TikTok is becoming the social media of choice to many young people and adults (my wife loves it for Baby ideas). Video is undergoing a renaissance—whether for news, entertainment, or education, people are flocking to it for their content fix. Think about it: how many of you head to YouTube before even considering a Google search when you need to learn how to do something?

This shift is happening because people increasingly demand fast, engaging, and—most importantly—content they can control. At a 2019 conference, Gary Vee asked an audience how many still watch traditional free-to-air TV. Less than 1% raised their hands.

So, what does this tell us? People are selective with their time. If they're this picky with personal entertainment, you can bet they're equally discerning in the professional world on platforms like LinkedIn.

So, one of the best ways you can do that is? Keep it short and sweet.

LinkedIn Judgement – Gone in 60 Seconds

Research shows that the average video loses **20% of its audience within the first 10 seconds**, and by the 30-second mark, **33% of viewers** have clicked away. By 1 minute, a staggering **45% of viewers** have dropped off. According to **Wistia**, the sweet spot for videos on social media is between **1 to 2 minutes**—this range tends to have the highest engagement levels. With attention spans shrinking and so much content vying for attention, keeping your video under 60 seconds maximizes impact and ensures you hold onto your audience longer.

Here are some examples of successful under-60-second videos in the media that illustrate the power of brevity:

1. **TikTok Challenges**: Many TikTok creators use short-form challenges to engage viewers quickly. For example, the *"Savage Love"* dance challenge features short choreography tutorials that are easy to follow, often under 30 seconds, and have gone viral, garnering millions of views.
2. **Instagram Reels**: Brands like **Dunkin' Donuts** and **Chipotle** have effectively utilized Instagram Reels, creating engaging promotional videos that highlight menu items or special deals in under 60 seconds. Their concise storytelling keeps audiences engaged and encourages sharing.
3. **YouTube Shorts**: Creators like **Zach King** have mastered the art of storytelling in under 60 seconds. His magic video tricks often deliver punchy surprises and clever edits, making them highly shareable and appealing to viewers looking for quick entertainment.
4. **Facebook Ads**: Companies like **BarkBox** create captivating ads under 60 seconds showcasing their subscription service. By focusing on engaging visuals and concise messaging, they effectively convert viewers into subscribers.

5. **Snapchat Stories**: Brands such as **Nike** use Snapchat to create short, engaging stories that highlight new products or campaigns, often featuring quick glimpses of athletes or influencers, all in under a minute.

Observing the Law

When we first started creating video content at Legal Home Loans, our debut video was a whopping seven minutes long. Unless you are posting to YouTube, seven-minute videos have no place on LinkedIn, unless low engagement is the goal. It was a valuable learning experience that led us to trim our videos. Over time, we trimmed our videos down to 3 minutes, then 2 minutes, and finally the magical sub-1-minute mark.

As the videos got shorter, engagement shot up. People appreciated the brevity, and I still stick to the 60-second rule today for maximum impact.

Engagement Tip:

According to LinkedIn, video views are counted after 3 seconds. To gauge true engagement, it's recommended to multiply the number of views by 100, as this reflects the number of viewers who watched the video for at least that duration. This metric can help you understand the actual reach and impact of your video content.

Recently, with the rise of TikTok, YouTube Shorts, and Instagram Reels, I've noticed that posting short videos or stories—often just 1 to 5 seconds long—can lead to a significant boost in engagement. While this quick format captures attention easily and reduces the likelihood of viewers skipping, it may sometimes lack depth or substance in terms of educational value. Nevertheless, these bite-sized clips can be effective for building brand presence, omnipresence and adding a fun element to your content strategy.

Pro Tip #1 – Homemade Over Polished

In my experience, LinkedIn's algorithm tends to favor authenticity. I've found that highly polished corporate videos often get downgraded, while handheld, raw footage receives a boost. Viewers are more inclined to engage with content that feels genuine. Plus, it's much more efficient for me—I can shoot 5 to 10 short, authentic videos in just 10 to 15 minutes, compared to spending hours on a polished production.

Pro Tip #2 – Essential Gear

If you are creating videos or conducting interviews from a computer, whether it is a Mac or PC, there are three essential tools you should consider investing in:

- **Ring Light:** The Neewer Ring Light is a great option for even, professional lighting that enhances video quality.
- **Camera**: The Logitech StreamCam provides excellent video quality, but if you prefer convenience, your iPhone camera can also deliver impressive results.
- **Speaker**: For clear, professional sound, the Yeti microphone is a solid choice, but if you're looking for even crisper audio, the Rode NT-USB is another great option.

Pro Tip #3 – Cut & Print

If you can get your hands on software like FinalCut Pro or Premier I can attest to our success on LinkedIn and business in the early days because of this program. It elevates our video quality and makes our content stand out. This software allows you to add banners, sound effects, subtitles, and adjust video contrast, making your content pop across platforms like LinkedIn and Instagram.

Pro Tip #4 – Get on the Tok!

If you're unable to purchase these programs, do yourself a favour and download TikTok and start an account. As my role in our company has expanded and the demands on my time continue to grow and grow, I have less time to invest into content editing. Short on time too? TikTok is a lifesaver. You can quickly cut, style, and share a 60-second video in less time than it takes to edit on professional software like Final Cut Pro. Plus, you can easily repurpose TikTok content on Instagram, Facebook, and LinkedIn.

Pro Tip #5 – Gear Up Checklist:

Get Your Equipment Sorted:

1. **Microphone:** Ensure you have a high-quality microphone for clear audio.
2. **Ring Light:** Use a ring light for flattering, even lighting in your videos.
3. **Background Lighting:** Consider soft background lighting to enhance the visual appeal.

4. **Personal Objects:** Include meaningful objects in your background to convey your personality and brand story.
5. **Editing Software:** Final Cut Pro (or your preferred video editing software) for professional editing.
6. **Tripod/Selfie Stick:** Stabilize your shots with a sturdy tripod or selfie stick.
7. **AirPods (or headphones):** For monitoring audio quality during recording and editing.

Additional Considerations:

- **Camera:** Consider using a DSLR or high-quality webcam for better video quality.
- **Backdrop:** Ensure your recording space has a clean, professional backdrop.
- **Green Screen:** If you plan on using virtual backgrounds, a green screen can enhance production quality.
- **Batteries/Power Bank:** Keep extra batteries or a power bank handy for long recording sessions.
- **Storage:** Have adequate storage, like external hard drives or cloud storage, for your video files.
- **LED Light Signs:** Use LED light signs that reflect your brand for an engaging touch

Transgressing the Law

I often see companies sharing highly polished videos on LinkedIn, and the reactions from their networks are often underwhelming. For instance, a well-known marketing agency posted a slick, corporate-style video showcasing their services, and it received minimal engagement.

Meanwhile, a small startup shared a casual behind-the-scenes clip of their team brainstorming ideas—raw and unedited—and it went viral within their niche.

Ask yourself this: do you sit and listen to the ads on YouTube? I rest my case. People crave authenticity, and they can easily spot when something feels overly produced. Individuals who don't make the effort to film genuine, relatable content will soon be left behind in this fast-paced digital landscape.

As Ryan Holiday emphasizes in *Perennial Seller*, the essence of great content lies in its ability to connect with audiences on a deeper level. Highly polished productions often lack the raw honesty that fosters real engagement. The viral success of that small startup's video illustrates this perfectly: they shared not just a product, but a relatable experience that resonated with their audience. This is the power of storytelling. It's not about crafting the perfect message but rather about conveying authenticity and vulnerability.

Moreover, in his other book *Growth Hacker Marketing*, Holiday advocates for experimentation and adaptation. Don't shy away from trying different approaches; the data you gather will inform what resonates most with your audience. Embrace the discomfort of being yourself on camera; it's where the real connections happen. Authenticity is not just a buzzword—it's a fundamental principle for sustainable growth. In a landscape saturated with polished, impersonal content, those who dare to be genuine will stand out and foster meaningful relationships with their audience.

LinkedIn Live – The Exception to the 60-Second Rule

Once you are on LinkedIn's radar, you will have the opportunity to request access to LinkedIn Live. This feature significantly challenges the 60-second rule, allowing for live videos ranging from 15 minutes to an hour. Streamyard is a popular tool for streaming on LinkedIn Live, and it's perfect for interviews or informal chats.

I encourage you to apply for LinkedIn Live access and set up conversations with colleagues or, even better, your clients. Focus on topics like their business journeys and how they've achieved their success. They'll appreciate the spotlight, and you'll be directing attention and potential business their way. Remember, energy flows where attention goes.

See my Live with Cullen Haynes series on Spotify or Apple for an example of LinkedIn Live. https://podcasts.apple.com/au/podcast/live-with-cullen-haynes/id1639782288

Streaming on LinkedIn Live accomplishes two key things: it positions you as an expert with the social media savvy to engage live audiences, setting you apart from the typical polished corporate videos. Additionally, it gives you the chance to interview clients and guests, allowing their expertise and charisma to reflect positively on you.

Live with Cullen Haynes. LawLive Episode #44 with Barrister & Legend Darren Mort

Pro Tip #6 – Repurpose & Recycle

One of the most effective strategies for maximizing your content is repurposing. For instance, take the audio from your LinkedIn Live streams and upload it as a podcast on platforms like Spotify or Apple Podcasts. This strategy allows you to transform one video into multiple content streams, significantly expanding your reach and engagement.

Many successful content creators utilize this approach. For example, **Gary Vaynerchuk** regularly records his keynote speeches and discussions, then repurposes them into podcast episodes. This not only broadens his audience but also allows his insights to reach listeners who prefer audio formats.

Similarly, **Pat Flynn** of Smart Passive Income often uses video content from his YouTube channel as the basis for his podcast episodes. By doing this, he effectively engages with both visual and auditory audiences, maximizing the impact of his content.

Another great example is **Joe Rogan**, whose podcast leverages video interviews shared on YouTube. While the full-length episodes are available on platforms like Spotify, the video clips are often repurposed as shorter content for social media, increasing his visibility across various platforms.

By repurposing your LinkedIn Live streams into podcasts, you can tap into new audiences and provide additional value to your existing followers. This multi-platform strategy not only enhances your content's longevity but also establishes your expertise across different mediums.

New Feature Just Dropped | October 2024

At the time of this writing, LinkedIn has dropped a new feature on your dashboard; the Video Feature. LinkedIn's new video feature, inspired by the short-form content model of TikTok, offers a fresh way to engage your audience, turning your profile into a dynamic personal brand. Unlike TikTok's playful, casual vibe, LinkedIn's platform calls for a more polished, professional tone, but with the same focus on concise, visually compelling content. These videos allow you to share insights, tips, or personal experiences in under 60 seconds, giving your audience a quick hit of value that can capture attention, increase engagement, and showcase your expertise.

For those unfamiliar with TikTok, here are some simple steps to help you film high-quality videos for LinkedIn's new feature:

- **Shoot in vertical mode**: Hold your phone upright for the best format compatibility with LinkedIn's new video feature.
- **Use good lighting**: Natural light works great, but if needed, invest in a ring light to ensure your face is well-lit.
- **Stabilize your camera**: Use a tripod or a steady surface to avoid shaky footage.
- **Plan your message**: Focus on one key point, keeping it concise and relevant to your audience.
- **Speak naturally**: Avoid reading from a script—talk directly to the camera as if you're speaking to a client, keeping the tone conversational.

- **Keep it professional yet engaging**: No need for flashy effects, but bring energy and personality to your delivery to make a strong connection.
- **Stick to short, impactful content**: Aim for under 60 seconds, ensuring your message is clear and valuable without overwhelming viewers.

Closing Thoughts: Lights, Camera, Action!

As we wrap up this chapter, remember that in the fast-paced world of LinkedIn, being engaging is non-negotiable. Embrace video as your trusty sidekick—your secret weapon to cutting through the noise and capturing attention. Whether you're sharing quick insights, celebrating milestones, or simply being your authentic self, let your personality shine through.

Just think about it: in a world full of polished ads and scripted speeches, authenticity stands out like a neon sign. So, grab your phone, light up that Neewer Ring Light, and get comfortable with being a little uncomfortable. Your audience is waiting, and they crave the genuine connection only you can provide.

And here's a challenge: the next time you think about hitting *"post,"* ask yourself—does this video add value? Is it engaging? Is it a true reflection of me? If you can answer "yes" to all three, you're on the right track!

Now go forth and create! Your next great video is just a click away, and who knows? It might just be the piece of content that propels you to the next level in your LinkedIn journey. Remember, every second counts—make them memorable!

Law #18 – Document, Don't Create: Business Is Personal

> Be *yourself.* Everyone else is taken.
> — Oscar Wilde

So, you've got your LinkedIn profile set up and your equipment ready. Now what? It can be daunting—I know it was for me at first. We all understand our businesses but when it comes to LinkedIn, Content reigns supreme. But therein lies another question, what content do you create? One of my legal clients, David Gale, framed this answer brilliantly. Read on dear reader.

LinkedIn Judgement – Life can be your content

In my podcast, **LawLive**, one of my guests, leading family lawyer David Gale—who coincidentally started his firm the same day we filmed and is a powerhouse on TikTok—shared his approach to content creation: *"Cullen, I subscribe to the philosophy of 'Document, don't create.' I don't sit down every day and think, 'What am I going to write or video about today?' Instead, I share what I'm doing or what's coming across my desk—day-in-the-life type of content. If I have an idea I want to post, I share it."*

This philosophy could serve you well, too. After all, no one can tell the story of your day-to-day life better than you can. So why not illuminate your experiences?

As Dr. Seuss famously wrote *"You are you. That is truer than true. There is no one alive that is youer than you."*

Observing the Law

Documenting personal experiences brings authenticity to your posts, which is key to engagement.

Make it personal! In another interview I did on ***LawLive***, I spoke with my dear friend Adrian Corbould who said *"Cullen, what I know from following you, is that you love to run, and get up early, F45 quite consistently. You also read quite prolifically that it insulates your walls. And you love meeting people, praising lawyers and your team and you put them on a pedestal and praise them, which is quite refreshing.*

Now by the same token, you can put post after post, day after day of Legal Home Loans and Finance and it would not make a dent. All the personal energy and enthusiasm that is visibly evident in your posts means that when I next need a loan or someone who does, I'll be recommending you."

Now I can hear the cacophony of LinkedIn critics: *"Business is business, and personal is personal—LinkedIn is not Facebook."* Yawn

I've got news for you. Business is personal and LinkedIn has evolved to a platform that has encouraged people to bravely show their real selves, not just the stuffy collateral and business posts that get no traction. Authenticity thrives. In a world filled with fake news and disingenuous content, people crave real connections. They want to see the individuals behind the companies.

For me, my life is all about *self-actualization* for others and myself, energy, and positivity so I keep my content aligned with these values.

Running – As an avid long-distance runner (Running is my therapy) I post my workouts, F45 clips and ruminations I've been pondering. Sometimes I even weave in finance and LHL content on the run.

Legends of Law – Lawyers, clients, and leading legal colleagues which I put on a pedestal and shout out along with a photo of them and me (more in Law #20)

Yes/No Polls – A very effective way to jack into one's emotions. I frame negatively but keep it positive. More on this in the next chapter.

Finance – As someone who helps lawyers with finance, I keep my 60-second videos entertaining, educational, and light—elevation through education.

LawLive/Live with Cullen Haynes – Excerpts from my podcast. I take little vignettes and snippets, and repurpose to bite size 60 second clips

PP – Personal Post/Self-Enrichment – Probably the most honest, raw, and real side of your profile, this is where people get to see the real you. I post something valuable, authentic, and unapologetically me. Having been blessed to be a father this year, I've been posting my journey You'd be surprised at how many people, both clients and new connections come out of the woodwork to wish me luck and give me their two cents worth. I even had one gentlemen take me to coffee and give me two books to help with our parenting journey.

People love giving their opinion, experience, and views on things, so if you're able to tap into that and elicit that, then your content will shine through.

80/20 Call to Action Rule - The Pareto Principle – It's important to balance value with promotion. No one likes to be preached or sold to.

For every sales post, share 4-5 value-driven posts. Remember, elevation through education. Remember, the 80% is why people follow you, and the 20% is for those ready to engage with your services. Lead with value first.

Book Reviews – Newsletter – As a self-confessed Bibliophile, that's a book fanatic to those unfamiliar, I take both photos of what I'm reading and then review the ones that have particularly piqued my interest. I use the article feature on LinkedIn. One year I read 115 books and reviewed as many as I can. I've recently converted the articles I've been reading into a newsletter using LinkedIn's very cool Newsletter function. It allows people to subscribe and will notify all of them when you write a new article. At current writing I've posted 31 reviews this year and gained 4,244 followers on my newsletter alone.

My 'Read, Rated & Reviewed' LinkedIn Newsletter.

So, what's the message here? Be yourself, even when the naysayers argue that business and personal should remain separate. LinkedIn is not Facebook the petty tyrants insist. But trust me, you'll forge stronger connections, and build more rapport with your tribe & clients if they get to see the heart behind the corporate face!

<u>Transgressing the Law – 80/20 Rule CTA Continued</u>

"Jab, jab, jab, jab – Right Hook" – Gary Vaynerchuk

To grow your business and drive revenue, you need a Call to Action (CTA). Otherwise, your educational content will fall flat. Gary Vaynerchuk likens creating value-driven content to throwing multiple jabs before delivering a right hook—your CTA.

It's what your tribe wants! They want to see you succeed. Did you know that only about 1% of people in any audience may be ready to engage with your product or service at any given time? To help your tribe elevate alongside you, focus on educating them with your valuable content (the jabs) before introducing your sales posts (the right hook).

This is what Adrian Corbould was talking about in my LawLive Episode #12, where he said that if I posted about finance and mortgages every day, he'd probably tune out and skip to next item in the feed. It's because I post about my life, books, running, Legends of Law, my son Benji, that he takes an interest and wants to genuinely know what I'm up to. And he'd recommend me more because of those things not the finance posts one expects from a broker anyway.

Don't fall into the trap—posting a CTA every day. This approach can alienate followers and potential clients. People are naturally resistant to being sold to around the clock, and I assure you, this strategy will do more harm than good.

I once purchased a cold calling book from a gentleman (who shall remain nameless) to improve my negotiation skills. The latter is what I wanted to improve. It taught you how to confidently call and talk to anyone about your service, product or offering. His posts were always flogging his book. He would often tag me along with 10 to 100 other connections, sharing his CTA-laden posts within the group and asking everyone to like, share, and comment. This tactic might have led to hundreds of likes in a short time, but at what cost?

One connection eventually called him out, saying, *"Hey X, I like you, but I don't appreciate being tagged and asked to like your posts; it feels a bit spammy. If it's okay, I'd like to ask you to stop."*

The silence that followed in that group was deafening. Don't be that person. Focus on adding value first. More importantly, I still haven't read his book four years later because of that interaction.

Pro Tip #1 – Frequency Matters

If you post as frequently as me, RE you post five times a day, then by the Pareto Principle (80/20) it's acceptable to include a CTA once daily. If you post once a day, limit CTAs to once or twice a week. Adjust the frequency based on your content strategy. It's all about the frequency in which you're adding value so apply the 80/20 rule to your own schedule and output.

Pro Tip #2 – Timing is Key

Choose optimal times for your CTAs to maximize engagement. From my experience, lunch breaks or commutes often yield the best results. Studies show that posting between 11 a.m. and 1 p.m. on weekdays can lead to higher interaction rates, as people tend to check their social media during their breaks.

If you post weekly, aim for Tuesday or Wednesday. This is when productivity is typically high, and professionals are more receptive to new ideas. Influencers like Gary Vaynerchuk often emphasize the importance of timing in his social media strategy, recommending that posts be timed to when your audience is most active.

For instance, *HubSpot* found that their highest engagement on LinkedIn came from posts made around noon and between 5 p.m. and 6 p.m. This aligns with the idea that people are checking their feeds during breaks or winding down for the day.

Consider your audience's habits and tailor your posting schedule accordingly. By strategically timing your CTAs, you can significantly increase your chances of being seen and engaged with.

Closing Thoughts: Be the Conversation Starter

As you navigate the dynamic landscape of LinkedIn, remember that the key to connecting with your audience lies in authenticity and timing. It's not just about broadcasting your message; it's about engaging with your community in a meaningful way.

So, next time you're tempted to post another CTA, pause for a moment. Ask yourself: "Am I adding value, or am I just trying to sell?" If you're genuinely offering something beneficial, your audience will respond. After all, nobody enjoys being bombarded with sales pitches 24/7. Instead, think of your LinkedIn presence as hosting a lively dinner party: you wouldn't want to be that guest who only talks about their latest product while everyone else is sharing stories and laughing!

LinkedIn is like a conversation, where engagement and value matter more than constant self-promotion.

And remember, each post is a chance to showcase your unique voice, your expertise, and yes, your personality. So, whether you're sharing a humorous anecdote from your day, a motivational quote that resonates with you, or a valuable lesson learned along the way, make it count!

As you embark on this journey, embrace the mantra of *"Document, don't create."* Let your experiences unfold naturally, and don't shy away from showing the real you. The world doesn't need another cookie-cutter professional; it needs your authentic story.

So go ahead—get out there, make some noise, and let your personality shine! Who knows? Your next post might just be the spark that ignites a powerful connection or even lands you a fantastic opportunity.

Keep it real, keep it fun, and above all, keep it you. Your tribe is waiting!

Law #19 – Polls of Persuasion: The Yes/No Paradigm

The oldest and shortest words 'Yes' & 'No' — are those which require the most thought.
— *Pythagoras*

When LinkedIn introduced the Polls feature, I became immediately hooked. Not only was it unique, but it also gave people the chance to voice their opinion—anonymously—while validating their argument to others.

Over the past few years, using polls has been the single biggest factor in my follower growth, with a daily increase of at least 5-10 followers. Polls are an incredible way to:

1. Engage with your network,
2. Rally your tribe, and
3. Train them into your worldview.

I post a poll daily, typically mid-morning to get maximum traction. But this raises the question: *What should you poll?*

You probably know what I'm going to say—don't force creativity. *Document, don't create.* For me, that starts during my morning run, followed by a shower and a scan of the *Financial Review*. Each day, I find poll ideas from articles that resonate with my tribe or spark thoughtful debate. (By the way, the *AFR* is truly the daily habit of successful people.)

For instance, at the time of writing this (October 2024), Australia has seen over 13 rate rises in 15 months, and the public is feeling the pinch.

The cost of living is increasing, and many people are facing the reality of their low fixed rates expiring—leading to potentially doubled or tripled repayments. As a broker working with risk-averse lawyers, this issue resonates strongly with my tribe so being able to vote on it in a poll is very on brand and engaging.

How to Frame Your Polls

Tony Robbins says, *"We rationalize with logic but make decisions based on emotion."* And nothing taps into the emotional centre of the brain faster than negatively-framed content. Now, while my brand is positive and uplifting, I don't shy away from the realities of human nature.

LinkedIn Judgement – If it bleeds, it leads 📰

There's an old saying in journalism: *"If it bleeds, it leads."* The idea is that people are more likely to pay attention when news disrupts their worldview. For instance, a headline like "Tornado Imminent: Devastation and Destruction to Come!" will grab far more attention than *"Sunny Days Ahead!"* This taps into the brain's limbic system, which triggers an emotional response and driving engagement because people naturally want to know how bad the damage will be and how it's going to affect them.

This phenomenon is backed by research in behavioural economics, which shows that loss aversion—the tendency to prefer avoiding losses rather than acquiring equivalent gains—plays a significant role in decision-making. A study by *Kahneman and Tversky (1979)* demonstrated that losses are psychologically about twice as powerful as gains. This means that when presenting information, framing it in a way that highlights potential loss can be more effective than focusing on potential gain.

In sales, fear can be a more powerful motivator than the promise of gain. People are more likely to act to avoid losing $10 than to gain it. For example, consider the classic marketing tactic of emphasizing limited-time offers. A campaign that states *"Only 3 Days Left to Save!"* often generates more urgency and responses than one that promotes a standard discount without a time constraint.

An anecdote to illustrate this comes from a well-known ad campaign in the late 1990s for a major insurance company. The commercials focused on the dire consequences of not being insured, with emotional storytelling that depicted families facing tragic scenarios. While some viewers found the ads distressing, they were incredibly effective at driving home the importance of coverage, resulting in a significant uptick in policy inquiries.

To make your content soar tap into emotion effectively. Whatever your content or question may be, frame it in a way that highlights potential challenges or threats. As I've found in my own work, when you position the question negatively, it often sparks more engagement and discussion.

Observing the Law

For example:

- *"Do you think rates will rise more?"* is softer and less effective than
- *"Are you stressed about the RBA continuing to raise rates?"*

Or:

- *"Do you like sunny days?"* versus
- *"Do you hate it when it rains?"*

You'll want to set your polls for two weeks to maximize reach, to adjust the duration before posting. After the poll is live, add your own view in the comments to spark further discussion.

Engagement isn't solely about likes or votes; it's about comments. That's where the real conversation happens.

A word of caution: framing your polls negatively taps into people's emotional responses—their "lizard brain," as it's often called. When you do this, brace yourself for an influx of comments, and some may leave you scratching your head, thinking, *"Did they really just write that?"* It will definitely bring out the crazies.

Regardless of whether the responses are good, bad, positive, or negative, engagement equals attention. And as Grant Cardone famously says, *"Love me or hate me, at least now you know me."* Run your polls right, and people will definitely know you.

The Paradox of Choice – The Psychology of Yes/No

Here's where the strategy comes in. The questions I use in my polls are always **closed**, meaning they prompt a simple Yes or No response. This choice is intentional. The goal is to make it easy for people to engage without thinking too hard. The less mental effort required, the more engagement you'll receive. I want people to feel compelled to vote, even if just to alleviate the tension my question stirs up. This often leads to likes, reactions, and comments.

Yes, this approach may seem Machiavellian, but it works. the more options you provide, the lower the engagement will be. So, keep it simple. You actually want to subscribe to George Orwell's mantra in 1984 and ensure your tribe follow it – Don't Think.

Keep it simple, stick to Yes/No questions. You don't even need to focus strictly on your niche. Some of my best polls have been about movies, music, or pop culture because they're accessible to everyone. Variations like Happy/Sad or Hero/Villain also work well.

One of my favourites was: *"In a post-apocalyptic world, would you be a Hero or a Villain?"*

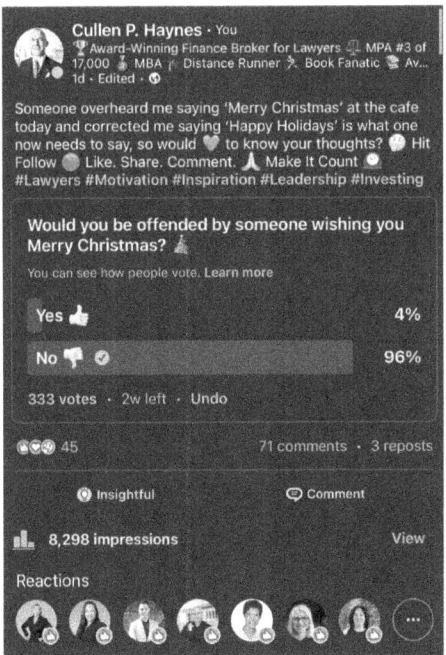

My ever-polarising Christmas Poll

Transgressing the Law

You'll know the uninitiated when you see their content. They make their lack of understanding obvious. They utilise polls as a means of research to have their network vote on multiple choice questions. I don't have a penchant or love of these, in fact I see ABCD questions as form of psychometric testing. And as such, to be avoided at all costs. Usually, these polls offer shallow, basic market research type questions and what's more non-engaging and overtly simple choices: -

"What's your favourite fruit?"

- Apples
- Bananas
- Strawberries
- Grapes

The obvious problem with the above it, it's not something that many people care about. It's trite, broad, vague, and polling for polling's sake. Other common missteps include asking:

"What's your favourite day of the week?"

- Monday
- Tuesday
- Wednesday
- Friday

Avoid this trap at all costs. You're better than that.

The Winning Poll Template

Follow this template to maximize engagement:

1) Start with a real conversation you've had with someone in your network, like:
   "Had a great chat with a lawyer friend over ☕ about whether passion should lie in work or outside of it."
2) Then ask:
   "What are your thoughts? 🤔"
3) Sign off with a call to action and your hashtags
   "Hit Follow 🔘 Like. Share. Comment. 🙏 Make it Count 📷 #Lawyers #Motivation #Inspiration #Leadership #Career"

Pro Tip #1 – Real Talk & Social Proof

I always try to tie my poll to a recent conversation I've had with someone from my tribe. This approach shows that you actively engage with your network. Alternatively, you can relate it to an article, book, or event you've experienced. This sets the tone that your poll is real, raw, and timely.

Why does this work?

There's a psychological concept known as *social proof*, which suggests that people are more likely to engage when they see that others, especially within their network, are involved. When you frame your poll around a recent conversation with someone in your tribe, it signals that you're actively connected and engaged with your audience. This encourages others to participate because they perceive it as relevant and part of an ongoing discussion.

Anecdotally, many LinkedIn influencers, including Gary Vaynerchuk, often mention that referencing real conversations or events increases engagement because it adds a layer of authenticity. People want to be part of something *"in the moment."* You're not just posting generic content; you're curating a conversation that is active, immediate, and engaging.

Pro Tip #2 – Would ♡ to know

I keep the question simple by asking, *"Would love to know your thoughts?"* I never share my own view in the pre-poll body because I don't want to influence my tribe's vote or skew the results.

Why is this important?

Extensive research supports this approach: sharing your opinion upfront can lead to *anchoring*, where people subconsciously latch onto the first piece of information they hear, influencing their own response. This can create bias in the results, making them less authentic. Additionally, *confirmation bias* kicks in when people seek out information that aligns with your initial opinion, rather than forming their own independent views.

By holding back your opinion until after the poll, you encourage more honest engagement and get a truer sense of what your network thinks.

Pro Tip #3 – The Sign-Off Strategy: Familiarity Breeds Engagement

Maintain a consistent sign-off across all posts. I recommend something simple but effective like:

Hit Follow 🏐 *Like. Share. Comment.* 🙏 *Make it Count* 📩

Then, include relevant hashtags such as #Lawyers #Motivation #Inspiration #Leadership #Career. This should be a standard practice for every post.

Why?

Repetition is crucial for social media success. Research highlights the *mere-exposure effect*, which shows that people tend to develop a preference for things they are repeatedly exposed to. Consistently repeating your call to action and hashtags increases the likelihood of engagement because your audience becomes more familiar with your message over time.

Additionally, consistent messaging builds trust. When your tribe sees the same sign-off and hashtags, it reinforces your brand, making you more memorable. Repetition isn't just about being noticed—it's about being remembered.

Pro Tip #4 – Your View Counts

Put your views in the comments so people know where you stand. For example, you might say, "I voted yes, and this is why…"

Why is this effective?

Sharing your views in the comments encourages a deeper dialogue. Behavioural psychology research shows that articulating opinions enhances commitment, they become more committed to them—a phenomenon known as the *commitment consistency principle*. This means that when you express your reasoning publicly, you not only clarify your thoughts but also encourage others to do the same.

Anecdotally, many successful LinkedIn users, like Adam Grant, often emphasize the importance of transparency in discussions. Grant frequently shares his thoughts in the comments of his posts, encouraging dialogue and enhancing his engagement. This practice not only positions you as a thought leader but also invites diverse perspectives, creating a richer discussion.

By placing your views in the comments, you also make it clear that you value input and are open to dialogue, which can lead to a more vibrant and engaged community around your content.

Pro Tip #5 – 2 Weeks Max

Always extend your polls out to two weeks to maximize the time available for votes.

Why is this effective?

Extending the duration of your polls allows more people to see and engage with them. *HubSpot* research shows that longer polling periods significantly boost participation, as it gives followers multiple opportunities to engage with your content, especially in a fast-paced platform like LinkedIn, where content is constantly being updated.

Anecdotally, many influencers, such as Neil Patel, advocate for longer polling durations to capture a wider audience. Patel often reports that polls lasting up to two weeks not only gather more responses but also lead to richer discussions, as more users have time to reflect and engage with the question.

Additionally, spreading out your polling period can help you reach different segments of your audience, as not everyone will be online at the same time. This approach not only boosts engagement but also helps you gain more insights into your network's opinions.

Pro Tip #6 – Come see the world like me

Use your questions to get your tribe thinking like you and seeing your worldview. For me, as a broker, Yes/No polls are my go-to for engagement, such as:

- Are you worried about rising rates?
- Is it important to have an expert on your side?
- Do you dislike Real Estate agents?
- Do you take criticism well?

Why this works:

Crafting questions that resonate with your audience encourages them to align their thinking with yours. According to a study published in the *Journal of Consumer Research*, people are more likely to conform to the opinions and behaviours of their peers when presented with questions that elicit agreement or disagreement. This phenomenon, known as the "social proof" effect, can significantly enhance engagement on social media.

Furthermore, as shown in a study by *Sprout Social*, content that reflects the interests and concerns of the audience tends to generate higher interaction rates. This means your questions should not only be relevant but also provoke thought and encourage self-reflection among your followers.

Influencers like Gary Vaynerchuk emphasize the importance of asking questions that spark conversation, noting that doing so helps build a community around shared values and experiences. When you get your audience to engage with your worldview, you foster a deeper connection and encourage them to become advocates for your ideas.

So, get out there. Poll now. Poll often. Poll me over!

Closing Thoughts: Polling for Connection, The Art of Engaging with your Tribe

As we wrap up this poll-tastic journey, remember polls are more than just a fun way to engage your network—they're your secret weapon for connection, insight, and influence. Think of them as the digital equivalent of sharing a cuppa with a friend, where everyone gets to voice their opinion, and you can sit back and enjoy the lively discussion that follows.

So, the next time you're tempted to scroll past your feed, pause! Imagine the conversations waiting to unfold if you simply ask the right question. Whether you're tapping into the collective wisdom of your tribe or sparking a friendly debate, polls offer a platform to amplify voices—yours and theirs.

As you embark on your polling adventures, channel your inner pollster and remember this golden rule: "In the land of social media, it's not just about the votes you tally, but the connections you forge along the way."

Now, go forth and poll like the rock star you are! May your questions be thought-provoking, your responses be lively, and your comments section be a delightful mix of insights, laughter, and maybe even a little friendly banter. After all, the world is watching, so let's give them a show worth tuning into! 🎤✨

Law #20 – Circulate to Percolate: Elevate Others Above Yourself

We rise by lifting others.
— *Robert G. Ingersoll*

As old as the day is young, from *the Bible* to The Codex Gigas to the Bhagavad Gita to the current worshipped media like TikTok, Instagram and of course LinkedIn, shouting out the act of uplifting others has long been revered as a mark of respect and a way to harness the power of community. When you celebrate others, not only do you pay homage to their achievements, but you also create an opportunity for their success to reflect positively on you. This is a crucial aspect of this law that can significantly enhance your professional and personal relationships. One should not work for recognition or praise but do work worthy of recognition. Even better when you can piggyback on your colleagues and clients by praising their efforts—and having that shine come right back on you.

This law is one of my favourites because its implications extend beyond LinkedIn; it can transform your life and relationships in profound ways. By embracing the mindset of elevating others, you set off a ripple effect that can enhance both your network and your reputation. Prepare to feel the ripples!

The Psychology Behind Elevating Others

Drawing from Maslow's Hierarchy of Needs, this law satisfies several fundamental human desires. First, by placing someone else's achievements in the spotlight, you enable them to self-actualize and raise their profile. This directly fulfills their need for significance and self-esteem. Moreover, it fosters a sense of community: Love & Belonging, shifting the focus from "Me" to "We."

LinkedIn's algorithm seems to favour altruism by rewarding posts that emphasize lifting others with increased visibility. This means that when you promote your colleagues or clients, you not only elevate them but also enhance your own presence on the platform.

Three Methods to Elevate Others Above Yourself

<u>LinkedIn Judgement - Circulate to Percolate</u>

Whenever someone asks me about the key to success, I tell them: Circulate to Percolate – C2P. Those who know me well are familiar with this phrase, as I use it often and was originally gifted to me by my mentor at Macquarie Bank. He once told me a story about his favourite professor, who, at their final class, shared this cryptic yet powerful advice:

> *"When I finished university, my favourite professor walked into the room. It was the very last class before we all graduated from business school, and as he entered, a hush fell over the auditorium. We all understood that he only came out when he had something truly important to share, as he usually had his assistants lead the lectures. He approached the microphone, surveyed the room, and spoke.*
> *'So, you're about to go out into the world and make a name for yourselves. If there's one final piece of advice I can impart, it's this. Now, some of you may get it, but most of you won't, so I'm speaking to those who will...*

> *Circulate to Percolate.'*
> *With that, he walked off the stage. Mic drop — silence.*
> *These words stuck with me and still send chills down my spine."*

This philosophy has been the backbone of my approach since we launched Legal Home Loans. To capture the essence of my mentor's words, think of it like a percolator — a cylindrical apparatus, similar to a kettle with a plunger. Just as coffee infuses through the repeated circulation of water, building a richer flavour with each cycle, success in business comes through action, not stagnation. The more you "percolate" (circulate), the stronger the connections and results.

And for those in sales (or as Zig Ziglar famously put it, *"If you're dealing with people, you're in sales"*), momentum is key. If you truly want to generate potential leads, cultivate prospects, or engage your tribe, you need to get out from behind your desk and go face-to-face, belly-to-belly with your tribe.

Grant Cardone's insight in *The 10X Rule* resonates here: *"I spent a year organizing my business admin without calling on a single client. This was my mistake."*

So, get out there, circulate, and brew the best cup of success!

On stage and out with my tribe at Alistair Marshall's Legal Services & Supplier Conference April 2024

#LegendOfLaw – My Personal Shout Out Process

Many people who know me, know me as either the Finance for Lawyers Guy or the LinkedIn Guy. And feel that I'm everywhere all the time, always meeting people, always having coffee. Omnipresent. Some jokingly ask, *"Do you even work?"* The answer is yes, but my version of productivity thrives on face-to-face connections.

Pro Tip #1 – See and Be Seen

I also have a rule, there's no point having a coffee with someone if no one else can see you. See and be seen is the name of the game. You want to be in a space where you create serendipitous encounters with your tribe. That's why for my coffee meet ups (and my Calendly location) it's always the same place, Beanbah, a coffee shop, near the supreme court. Why? Because Lawyers, Barristers and Judges go there regularly.

I know all the names of the staff, the menu and am there pretty much every day. I'll even go there when I don't have a meeting, for the same reason. Just be seen.

I cannot tell you how much extra business I've been able to bring in just because I have those casual interactions with prospective clients who say *"Cullen, I've been meaning to speak with you – let's do coffee on ___ "*

The perception that I'm everywhere creates a powerful narrative. LinkedIn amplifies your reach; when people see you with others in their feed, it builds trust and familiarity.

So, pick a café or restaurant where your tribe gathers. Be seen and be seen often. I promise you'll be happy — and so will your bottom line.

That said, the fact that clients feel like I'm all places at once and that I know everyone in the legal world may or may not be true, however it's the story I curate and present to the world. And LinkedIn is a force multiplier because if people see your face often enough in the feed with other people, they know it starts to stick that, hey I like Jo, and Jo's with Cullen. I must then in turn like Cullen. Simple, yes. Powerful? Absolutely.

This omnipresent phenomenon is not an accident, and I work for it dearly. Here's my secret…read on dear reader.

LinkedIn Judgement – Take the Online, Offline

Many people will disagree with my assertion, but I will stand by it as it's made our company millions of dollars. The whole point of LinkedIn is to take the Online, Offline. That's it. Simple. In a nutshell. Connecting digitally is just the beginning; real connections are forged in person. As my mentor once told me, calls and teams can only do so much, when you meet someone offline, face to face, it takes you to another emotional level. And it's so true.

Reflect on your closest moments with your clients, friends, or family— were they formed over Zoom or in person?

So, you've followed the steps laid out up to this point. Your tribe member has accepted meeting for coffee. You're with them and may have already if there are any holes in their network are and what 3 people you can introduce them to (next Chapter). Now the fun begins.

My next question, before asking for the bill — always offer to pay and insist, is *"Would you be against a photo for LinkedIn because I'd love to get more connections and engagement for you?"* Because of the psychology, we've already covered, I very rarely if ever have someone say no.

Pro Tip #2 – Taking the Perfect Shot

While you might feel confident in taking selfies, here's how to master the perfect shot:

- **Choose a dynamic background:** Capture the café logo or a vibrant setting.
- **Engage with the camera:** Focus on the lens, not your reflections.
- **Point to the person you're with:** Highlight them in the shot.
- **Smile!**

Once you've taken your shot, ask them. *"Is there anything in particular you'd like me to say in our post? Or elevator pitch"* This fosters engagement and makes them feel valued. Some may be open and flexible with what you write. Others may be very specific. Either way, they'll love you for it.

Because I work for lawyers, here's my non-trademarked #LegendOfLaw post

1) 🫶 Why do I love LinkedIn? 🤗
2) Because I get to shout out #LegendsOfLaw ⚖️ like [Name]. This juggernaut wears many hats: Barrister, Advocate, Coder, Entrepreneur, and Technology Savant. Having founded Australia's leading legal marketplace, Rightful, he's on a mission to change the way law is delivered.
Always love catching up for a crafty brew at Beanbah ☕
Check it out now 😊 💻 [link]
3) If you're not connected, remedy this now 🤝
Why do you love 🤍 LinkedIn all? 🤗
4) Hit Follow ⚫ Like. Share. Comment. 👏 Make it Count 🧿
#Lawyers #CirculateToPercolate #Motivation #Leadership

Why does this post work and result in many new connections and new opportunities? Like all my posts, there's of course method in the madness:

1) **The algorithm loves positivity:** By expressing love for LinkedIn, I position myself favourably. Subtle, overt, or otherwise it works. If it gives me the edge, so be it!
2) #LegendsOfLaw – Recognizing others fosters reciprocity. Telling the world who they are and why I appreciate them gives others the reason to do the same – Also, it has the halo effect of that person's shine rubbing off on me too.

3) ***"Remediate this now"*** – Becomes a playful invitation for connection. This is a purple cow which people love me for. I've had clients connect with the person I shout out and write "Remediated"

4) **Repetition builds awareness:** Consistently engaging in this manner grows your network.

#LegendOfLaw Chris Dobbs | The Fintech Barrister | Outside of Beanbah (Legal Haunt)

Pro Tip #3 – Copycats welcomed

Do not vex yourself when you see others in your network adopting your newfound content creation and output. You'll have the pretenders emulate you or at least give it their best shot — and that's a *good* thing. Only recently, I had a marketer DM me, *"Cullen, I'm in marketing and do you mind if I steal your idea and do #LegendOfMarketing shout outs?"*

You know what my response was? An emphatic yes. Of course I don't mind. Imitation is the sincerest form of flattery.

To recap, posts like these elevate the other person and put them on a platform. The benefits are huge:

- You'll both see your connection and follower count grow, as your network sees them, and theirs sees you.
- Their reputation and shine will reflect back on you. People will reach out saying, *"Hey, I didn't know you knew X!"* This happens to me all the time — it's a powerful tool for connection.
- It shows you're a mover and shaker — present everywhere at once. Omnipresent.

Pro Tip #4 – Be sure to Use Portrait Mode

If you use Portrait Mode, on your iPhone or smartphone, you have a very engaging background that gives depth to you and your guest. Colour or unique architecture works and for that matter, natural beauty like gardens, trees, or foliage work well too. The more engaging, the better. It adds vibrancy. A bank manager I work with recently told me that he loves my posts with other people because they have, and I quote, *"So Much Joy!"* And they make him happy. This made me smile and made the last 5 years' worth it. Because this affirmation fuels my philosophy: **"To leave people better than I found them."**

#LawLive

I will shout out the streaming platform, Streamyard, which seamlessly integrates with LinkedIn Live. Check out StreamYard: **https://streamyard.com/pal/d/5229683975913472**

Here's why it's invaluable:

Why?

1) **Built for interviews:** Perfect for raising the profiles of your tribe.
2) **Live, multi-channel broadcasts:** Reach audiences on various platforms simultaneously. X, LinkedIn, Insta, Twitch, Facebook, YouTube.
3) **Pre-scheduling events:** Build anticipation and engagement.
4) **Content creation:** Download soundbites and videos for sharing across social media. Download the video footage and cut, share, and get all over your socials. I break up into little 60 seconds videos and use Final Cut Pro & TikTok when I'm in a rush to edit and share on LinkedIn, Insta, Facebook and YouTube too.
5) **Start a podcast:** Streamyard simplifies the process, allowing you to create engaging audio content. The instant nature of Streamyard (being able to download the audio and video) with

a bit of polish can be cut quite nicely into a podcast. So, starting a podcast while building a following has never been easier.

I've started 3 so far using this method and my tribe love it and tell me they really enjoy it too.

Observing the Law

"Edward Zia, a master influencer, exemplifies the 'Elevate Others' strategy. He played a significant role in helping me embrace my unique persuasion skills to uplift others. Here are some of the ways Ed effectively applies this approach:

- **Max Love Posts**: He often shares posts expressing admiration for others, giving them a spotlight.
- **LinkedIn Live Interviews**: Ed regularly conducts interviews with clients and peers, offering them a platform to share their expertise.
- **Friday Meetups**: Ed, a true savant at networking, hosts regular meetups where attendees can pitch their ideas and promote their business in a one-minute spotlight.
  - His ambassador role often grants him exclusive perks, allowing him to bring even more value to his community.
- **The Vault**: Through a subscription model, Ed offers exclusive content—interviews, videos, and valuable insights from his LinkedIn certification—accessible only to his inner circle.

I strongly recommend you like, share, and follow Ed.

Yes, you see what I did here—elevating someone in my book!

Pro Tip #5 – Sharing Across All Platforms

When it comes to content, the golden rule is this: don't limit yourself to just one platform. Share your posts across LinkedIn, Instagram, Facebook, X (formerly Twitter), and YouTube for videos. This gives your content the broadest possible reach and ensures you're meeting your audience where they are.

However, when it comes to platforms like Facebook/Meta, there's a catch. It's widely reported that their algorithm actively deprioritizes content that includes overt calls-to-action like *"Like, Share, Comment, Follow."* Why? Meta's business model thrives on paid advertising, so when posts seem too promotional or sales-driven, they're downranked in the news feed in favour of more "organic" content. The goal here is for Facebook to encourage businesses to pay for exposure.

A notable example comes from social media experts like Neil Patel, who emphasize that Facebook's algorithm favours personal engagement and authentic interaction over anything that feels like a direct sales pitch. Patel advises removing overt CTA phrases in organic posts to increase reach and engagement, rather than letting the algorithm squash it.

From my own experience, when we initially launched Legal Home Loans, we noticed that our Facebook posts that included *"Like, Share, Comment"* language were consistently underperforming. Once we adjusted our messaging to be more conversational and less sales-oriented, our engagement and reach improved significantly. It was a small tweak, but it made a huge difference.

The takeaway? Share broadly but adapt your messaging to each platform's specific nuances. Play by the rules of the algorithm—especially on platforms like Facebook/Meta—and watch your content circulate more effectively.

Transgressing the Law – The Humble Brag

If elevating others is one side of the spectrum, then the humble brag is its direct opposite. And unfortunately, LinkedIn has become a notorious playground for these self-congratulatory, veiled attempts at self-promotion.

At first glance, you might think that a humble brag is a clever way to raise your profile while giving a shout-out to your team or clients. On paper, it sounds good—you're recognizing their hard work, right? But here's the thing: audiences can easily see through these thinly veiled attempts at self-aggrandizement. What should be a celebration of collective success often comes across as fake, forced, and inauthentic. You know the one's especially when there's an award nomination or win that's just occurred. My friends at *Momentum Media* are quite adept at this with their Award Nominations across multiple industries and sub-categories (*Women in Law, Partner of the Year, Australian Law Awards* etc…)

Research shows that humble bragging can actually backfire. A study by *Harvard Business School* revealed that people who humble brag are perceived as less likable than those who engage in straightforward boasting. Why? Because humble brags come across as disingenuous. The attempt to mask self-promotion as modesty creates a disconnect between what you're saying and what people perceive. Simply put, humble bragging doesn't fool anyone and can erode trust.

We've all seen the classic example:

> "I can't believe I got nominated. #Blessed #Grateful. This nomination not only for me, but the team"

Let's be honest: most of these nominations are self-submitted, and the overt display of humility feels more like theatre than sincerity. It also is very disingenuous. *"I can't believe I won [for this self-nominated award I voted myself for"* Despite their efforts to recognize the team, the underlying message is all about self-promotion, and it's painfully transparent.

Allow me to share an example. I once saw a Partner, after winning a *"Partner of the Year"* award, post a cringe-inducing statement: *"I won!"* That's it. Just two words followed by an extended monologue on why he was so incredible. I'm still cringing from that post to this day. I don't think I'll ever recover. The worst part? The award was again self-nominated, and nothing screams *"Look at me!"* more than a self-congratulatory post for an accolade you essentially awarded yourself.

Take this as a cautionary tale. Don't fall into the trap of outsourcing these posts to your marketing team either—it doesn't help your authenticity. Believe me, audiences can tell when something's been crafted by a PR team. Genuine engagement builds connection; hollow self-praise erodes it.

The takeaway here: authenticity wins every time. If you're truly grateful for something, celebrate it genuinely—give real credit where it's due, without the need for self-glorification.

See below a funny meme I found that I know you'll love too:

Reality vs LinkedIn

Reality: I got my Driving License

LinkedIn: I'm honored and thrilled to announce that I have been selected among the top 5 applicants who participated in the professional and most respected exam which evaluates the skill and ability to operate fuel-based vehicles. I cannot wait to see what the next chapter holds, and I cannot express my appreciation to the **ministry of transportation, Google, NASA, and My neighbors** who supported me during this challenging journey.

Reality vs. LinkedIn (You know we've all done it)

Closing Thoughts: Authenticity Over Acclaim

In the world of LinkedIn and personal branding, the temptation to engage in humble bragging or self-promotion is always present. But remember authenticity wins over accolades. People connect with real, genuine stories, not with staged performances of success. If you're truly grateful for something—whether it's a win, a nomination, or recognition of your team—express that gratitude sincerely. Don't mask it behind false humility.

By elevating others and contributing to your community in meaningful ways, you'll build trust, respect, and a reputation that speaks far louder than any award or hashtag. In the end, your actions, not your accolades, will be the true measure of your influence.

Be bold. Be real. But most importantly, be yourself.

Law #21 – Pay It Forward: The Rule of Reciprocity: Elevate Your Influence by Connecting Others

Give, give, give, give, give...then ask.
— Gary Vaynerchuk

This law has been transformative for our business, opening countless opportunities and generating more revenue than any other principle outlined in this book. Why is this the case? This law aligns with the Law of Reciprocity. People are more inclined to return favors when they receive value first. Gary Vaynerchuk's philosophy of giving emphasizes the importance of serving others before seeking a sale.

After an initial coffee meeting, if you follow up by connecting a prospect with three individuals who can add value to their network, they will often feel compelled to reciprocate. This fosters a mutually beneficial relationship, enhancing your reputation.

LinkedIn Judgement – Bought, Not Sold

In the world of selling, it may sound counterintuitive, but people don't want to be sold to; they want to feel that they are making a purchase decision. As often attributed to Maya Angelou, *"People don't care how much you know until they know how much you care."* Her point about caring is crucial for LinkedIn networking, where connection and trust come first.

A powerful short film titled **A Joy Story: Joy & Heron** perfectly illustrates this concept. https://www.youtube.com/watch?v=ZQGuVKHtrxc The brief tale tells the story of a dog and his master in a calm lake at sunset.

The master is fishing, and his dog is dutifully watching, waiting for him to make a catch. Until a bird decides to crash the party and start stealing the master's worms. The dog growls, barks and proceeds to fight the bird every time and loses, only to be told off by his master who doesn't see the mischief happening unnoticed.

The dog feeling dejected, watches the bird fly over to its nest who has three chicklets: she's a mother. The birds are unable to eat the fish which were previously found. So, the dog offers the bucket of worms which the mother bird, takes, and feeds them to her little babies. Just when you think that's the end of our tale, and the dog feeling good that he's helped but guilty because he let his master down, the bird arrives with all the fish she'd caught that the babies won't eat. The master is elated, and the dog receives much love and praise as they won't need to fish for some time

Why am I including this story in a book about LinkedIn networking? Because so often we're like the master and the dog, We're often like the dog, focused on guarding what we want, instead of being generous. When we start from a place of generosity, the rewards—both tangible and intangible—will flow back to us, often in abundance.

And, circling back to Maya Angelou, what better way to show you care about the other person, your prospective client, than by giving. This mindset shift from scarcity to abundance is crucial in building genuine connections.

By introducing your prospects to like-minded individuals who can help them grow personally or professionally, you not only enhance your reputation but also stimulate the reciprocity effect. They will be more likely to either do business with you or refer you to someone who can.

In my business of finance and mortgages, I'm usually sitting down for coffee with a potential legal client. For those who haven't immediately indicated they are interested in a loan (even the ones that do) I always think about how I can add value by introducing them to others in my network.

The introductions should be context-sensitive; for instance, if they're a sole trader or business owner, they might benefit from connections with referral partners, top-notch marketers, financial planners, or accountants.

If they're a salaried graduate, senior associate, Partner drawing a wage, perhaps an introduction to an elite recruiter who can coordinate a strategic career play or at the very least have them secure a better salary. It doesn't really matter whether they take up the introductions, the very fact that you've shown bias for action and coordinated with no expectation of business in turn will be enough, trust me. It shows others that *"this person cares about the growth of myself and my business."* I've seen this time and again—your efforts will be reciprocated.

How to Execute This Law

I hear this question often, dear reader. Now given that you're reading a book on LinkedIn networking, do you think, call, text or email will suffice? Of course, not we're going to utilise LinkedIn itself. But I'm getting ahead of myself. To ask or not ask the permission firstly, that is the question. Instead of overcomplicating things with unnecessary questions, I see both as correct and if you choose the former, pre-framing yourself as someone who ads value first, is paramount. It shows them you're thinking about their needs and what's important to them.

When it comes to asking for permission, framing your request tactfully is essential. Remember, keep it simple. Here's a simple question I ask:

"Who in your field do you need to be connected to right now? I have a rule that I introduce three winners to help you win big; it's a bit of a religious thing for me." That last part usually brings a laugh and lightens the mood.

This question is likely one of the first times your prospect has encountered someone who offers to facilitate introductions so readily. It's a standout, a *"Purple Cow"* moment. Ask if you can take notes during your meeting, as it signals that you're invested in their success. If you already have names in mind for the introductions, share them in real time; they'll appreciate your proactive approach, as I'll show you shortly, dear reader.

If you need more time to think, promise to ruminate and follow up over (you guessed it) LinkedIn of course.

Pro Tip #1 – Connect on LinkedIn

Now that you've had a successful coffee, connect with the client over LinkedIn and ask that they accept request to introduce them (texting is usually a good prompt). As a rule, I make it a habit to connect with the client BEFORE coffee, that way they can do some backgrounds research and know what I look like.

Pro Tip #2 – Use Voicemails

You're going to use messages and the good old fashioned voicemail feature. If you're not connected already, this is a great excuse to connect and break the ice while you've already got their permission.

Open the messages, click the name of your client and the person you're introducing them too and hit that microphone button. It will automatically create a group.

Pro Tip #3 – What To Say…

You're ready to record. For this instance, I have John Solicitor, I'm connecting with Taylor a renowned recruiter. Here's my winning script to them both:

> *"Hey John, meet Taylor, Taylor meet John. As per our coffee, want to introduce you two powerhouses. John, Taylor is a leading lawyer who wants to make a dent in the legal universe. Taylor, John is a world class recruiter who'll be sure to make your impact heard all around Australia. I'll leave you both to it"*

Once you finish your recording, hit the 3 dots and press *"Leave the group"*

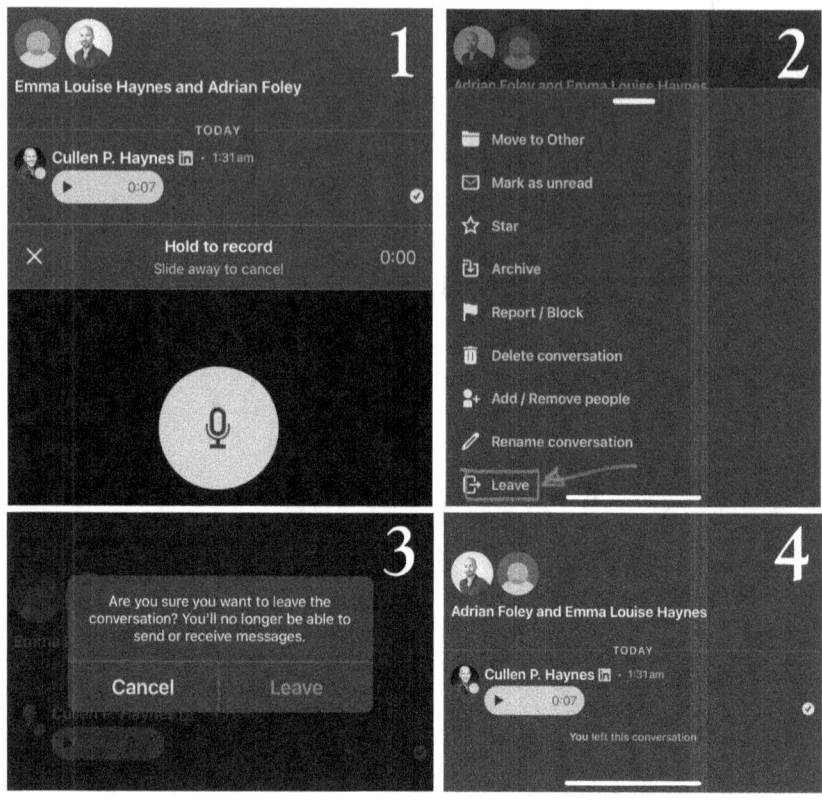

How to leave a group | Thanks to my wife & brother for volunteering

This step is crucial, as it provides them with privacy to discuss further, reinforcing the idea that you expect nothing in return.

This message works because it's an amalgamation of everything you've learnt thus far dear reader and addresses several human needs. Introducing someone to a prospective member of their tribe fulfills the need for significance and facilitating connections fosters community and self-actualization.

Pro Tip #4 – Never Decline a Coffee Invitation

Do this in meetings even when they're not your ideal target client. And DO NOT say no to coffees with anyone, ever. Period. End of story. Some of my biggest opportunities in business have come from meetings that weren't with my ideal customer. My old mentor once told me that everyone has a network of around 130 people. According to research from LinkedIn, each person can connect you to an average of 400 connections, meaning that every meeting could potentially open doors to a vast network. If you impress that non-prospect, they may introduce you to one, two, or even countless members of your ideal client base.

For instance, consider the story of a young entrepreneur, Lara, who attended a networking event and struck up a conversation with someone outside her industry. She wasn't expecting much from the meeting, believing it wouldn't lead to anything valuable. However, during their coffee chat, she discovered that this person was deeply connected to a non-profit organization in need of legal services.

Sarah offered her assistance, and not only did she gain a new client, but the non-profit also introduced her to several businesses that later became her ideal clients. This demonstrates the ripple effect of networking beyond your immediate circle.

Furthermore, a study published in the *Harvard Business Review* showed that relationships developed outside your immediate professional circle can lead to unexpected opportunities. This is known as *"The strength of weak ties,"* a term coined by sociologist Mark Granovetter, which suggests that acquaintances often have different social circles than close friends, leading to valuable new connections and opportunities.

So, dear reader, never say no to another coffee meeting again. You never know where it may lead!

Observing The Law

A great example of this principle in action is my friend Jon Sermon, one of Australia's top buyer's agents (he's English too, please don't hold that against him). Jon reached out to me via (wait for it...) LinkedIn and invited me to coffee.

One of the first questions he asked was, *"Who are the holes in your network?"* I was taken aback because I'd never been asked such a unique, value-adding question. I shared my need for law firms wanting to engage and add value to their employees through our Staff Benefits Program: where Big Law Firms (Top 50) get access to our service for free for their staff while we pay $1,000 on settlement of their loans. The next day, he introduced me to not just one, but three law firms. We continue to collaborate closely with them, and Jon still introduces me to law firms today while I continue to send clients his way.

So, who do you think I recommend to anyone looking for a house? The very British and dapper, Mr. Jon Sermon.

Transgressing The Law

A common mistake made by rookies and even seasoned professionals is to ask for introductions before giving. This approach creates a sense of obligation rather than generosity. Research by Robert Cialdini reveals that people are far more likely to return favours when they feel they've received something first. When individuals approach me with a transactional mindset, it stifles potential relationships.

I've had experiences where individuals have asked me to coffee and immediately transitioned to *"What can you do for me?"* This mentality stifles potential relationships.

I call it payback in reverse because, rather than feeling like a gift, it becomes a debt I owe. Never a good move when you want to create a relationship that lasts.

One financial planner took me to coffee and one of the first questions was, *"How many people are in your database, and how can I get access to them?"* Oof! At least buy me dinner first!

The fact that I can't recall his name underscores my point. Takers are never makers. Takers rarely success: givers always gain.

As Robert Kiyosaki, Author of *Rich Dad, Poor Dad* *"The more you give, the more you receive. The more you help, the more you get."*

Transgressing the Law: The Danger of Keeping Score

One of the most toxic behaviours in business relationships is the act of keeping score. Recently, a referral partner of ours kept an ongoing tally of the deals and opportunities he sent our way. He became frustrated and resentful when the referrals we sent him didn't convert as he expected. What started as a partnership based on mutual benefit quickly devolved into demands, accusations, and a sense of entitlement. Eventually, the relationship became so strained that my business partner and I had no choice but to part ways with him.

This situation perfectly exemplifies a key principle from Robert Greene's *48 Laws of Power*: *Law 13: When Asking for Help, Appeal to People's Self-Interest, Never to Their Mercy or Gratitude*. Greene illustrates through history that reminding people of the favours you've done for them almost always makes them angry. It stirs up resentment because it forces them to confront an uncomfortable truth—they are indebted to you. This partner's constant reminders of his "generosity" poisoned the relationship. Rather than fostering goodwill and collaboration, it bred frustration and animosity.

In business, it's essential to avoid the trap of keeping score. Strong relationships are built on trust, mutual benefit, and a shared understanding that not every transaction will lead to immediate rewards. Demanding more from a partnership based solely on a sense of entitlement will backfire, burning bridges rather than building them.

Closing Thought: "The Ripple Effect of Generosity"

As you leave each meeting, picture yourself casting a stone into a still pond. The ripples expand outward, reaching far beyond where the stone first touched the water. By connecting prospects with three people after every meeting, you're not just helping them; you're creating a network of opportunities that could come back around in unexpected ways.

Think of it like planting seeds in a garden. You may not see immediate results, but with time, those seeds will grow, flourish, and perhaps even bear fruit you never expected. Your generous act of connecting others can lead to collaborations, referrals, and friendships that enhance your professional landscape.

So, the next time you find yourself in a meeting, remember it's not just about the transaction at hand, but the vast network you're nurturing for the future. Who knows? That small gesture might be the spark that ignites someone else's success—and, in turn, your own.

Now go out there and create those ripples!

Law #22 – Book Yourself Solid & Command the Clock: Make Yourself Invaluable by Controlling Access

White space on your calendar is The Devil.
— Grant Cardone

I completely agree with Grant Cardone. When you glance at your calendar and see large expanses of white space, it's a clear signal that something is amiss. If that emptiness lingers, it can feel like you're trapped in a kind of hell. I've been there before—when we launched Legal Home Loans, I had no network, no prospects, and no clients. I had to get busy and start circulating to percolate. I had to get busy and start building connections to generate momentum.

"Yeah, Cullen..." I hear your collective groans. *"It's easy to say, invite prospects and referral partners to coffee, but you know how often they respond with, 'I'm not available at that time, what other times do you have?' until the conversation fizzles out or you forget to follow up."* I get it.

Back in 2018, I faced the same dilemma, dear reader. Fortunately, I found a solution through two key insights:

1) the psychological understanding that people are inherently lazy, and choose the path of least resistance
2) a handy little tool called Calendly.

Calendly: More Than Just Scheduling

Download it here: Calendly | https://calendly.com/cp-haynes-lhl/coffee virtual call

This app has truly transformed my life. I can honestly say I couldn't conduct business without it now.

I started, as everyone does, with the free version. I learned to navigate its nuances, exploring different calendar paths, times, and templates, before eventually upgrading to the paid version. I've never looked back. In fact, my entire company now uses Calendly, and I consistently recommend it to my busy legal clients who I want to see succeed.

I've progressed from crawling to running at full speed with Calendly. I now manage three different booking journeys: one for regular finance meetings, another for my LawLive podcast, and a third for general coffee chats—virtual or otherwise. I've truly maximized the benefits of this app, and the small monthly fee I pay is returned to me tenfold through saved time and increased revenue.

With a minimum of 8-10 meetings each day, staying on top of my schedule is essential. I lack the patience to babysit others through the scheduling dance of "When are you free?" Calendly allows me to fill my calendar with minimal effort.

As the name suggests, Calendly is more than a scheduling platform. It eliminates the hassle of back-and-forth emails and messages, while also automating workflows and managing various manual tasks.

Before diving into my Calendly game plan from soup to nuts, let's take a look at my initial email and message templates.

LinkedIn Judgement – Understanding Human Behaviour: People tend to avoid effort unless necessary

While we pride ourselves on efficiency and discipline, most of us (me included) naturally gravitate toward the path of least resistance. Another important phenomenon to consider is the *Paradox of Choice* (a great book by Barry Schwartz). The more options you present, the less likely someone is to make a quick decision—or any decision at all. Daniel Pink also addresses this in his *Masterclass* on Sales & Persuasion.

In one study, a jam salesperson in a shopping mall offered 26 flavours versus just two. The results showed that fewer options led to a significantly higher purchase rate. Sometimes, less truly is more.

People need guidance. Give them too many choices, and they'll lose interest or give up entirely. My old mentor used to say, *"A confused mind never makes a decision."* With that in mind, My *Book Yourself Solid* approach is designed to simplify the process.

> *"Hi there,*
> *Great that you're free for coffee. I have a great spot in mind, Benito's do the best pastries too. If you're not against it, how about Thursday or Friday at 10:15am. Alternatively, book in here https://calendly.com/cp-haynes-lhl/coffee_virtual_call"*

If you take away nothing else from this book, remember this message. It's been a time-saving goldmine and a significant revenue generator from meetings I otherwise might have missed.

Let's break it down. *"I have a great spot in mind, Benito's do the best pastries too"* As Zig Ziglar famously said, everyone is in sales. When you invite someone for coffee, you want them to anticipate the meeting and get excited about the location too.

"If you're not against it…" This phrase, inspired by Chris Voss in his compelling book *Never Split the Difference,* utilizes a psychologically framed question that elicits a positive response. Voss, a former FBI hostage negotiator, emphasizes the importance of tactical empathy in negotiations. This specific phrasing helps establish a collaborative atmosphere, making the client feel valued rather than as if they are merely doing you a favour.

Voss recounts a negotiation where he successfully turned a potentially contentious discussion into a positive dialogue by using similar framing techniques. By asking questions that presume a shared interest, he was able to build rapport and trust, paving the way for a more fruitful negotiation.

This approach sharply contrasts with traditional *"Get to Yes"* sales strategies, which often emphasize compromise at the expense of genuine connection. Instead of pushing for agreement, Voss's technique invites clients to explore options together, fostering a sense of partnership. Trust me, diving into Voss's insights will revolutionize your negotiation skills. But I digress.

"How about Thursday or Friday at 10:15 AM?" You might think it's redundant to offer two options when you already have a Calendly link. However, patience is key here. While millennials dominate the buyer landscape, many still have reservations about fully trusting technology, and they prefer the personal touch of direct communication. In fact, a recent survey by PwC found that 82%

of consumers want more human interaction in their purchasing decisions. By offering two specific time slots, you're not just relying on tech but creating a sense of personal engagement, which makes the interaction feel less robotic.

This is what I call the *"quick win"* strategy. By presenting two tailored options, you're simplifying the decision-making process for your clients and dramatically increasing the chances of a quick response. This approach avoids the back-and-forth hassle that often comes with scheduling. In my experience, 60 to 70% of people select one of the two time slots on the first try, especially when the personal touch of offering specific times makes it seem like you're speaking directly to them, not just automating a process.

The Magician's Choice in Sales

This technique reminds me of my early magician days and the Law of Equivocation, or *"The Magician's Choice."* In magic, it's a way of giving the illusion of free will while actually guiding the audience to a predetermined outcome. The same principle applies to meetings. You present two options, both of which lead to the same outcome—a confirmed booking. Whether they pick Thursday or Friday, you're still securing a meeting, all while maintaining control of the interaction. It feels like a collaborative decision for the client, but behind the scenes, you're steering the process.

I've applied this concept in sales over and over. One time, I was dealing with a senior partner at a prominent law firm who was notoriously hard to schedule. Offering two specific time slots felt like I was accommodating his schedule, while also giving the impression that I was in demand. Within minutes, I got a reply: *"Thursday works."* It was a win-win. If

I had just sent the Calendly link, he might have ignored it or delayed responding because it felt impersonal, but the personal offer of choice made all the difference.

Flexibility Without Inflexibility

Some may argue that offering just one option would simplify the process. While this may seem more efficient, my data suggests otherwise. When clients are presented with only one option, it often comes across as rigid or unaccommodating. They might think, "I'm not free at that time," and either delay responding or not respond at all. Offering two time slots, however, signals flexibility, even if those slots are the only ones you have available. According to research by *Cornell University,* people are more likely to engage when given choices, but not too many—two or three is optimal for quick decisions.

The beauty of this is that you can follow it up with: "Alternatively, book in here: [Calendly Link]." This streamlines the process for those comfortable with technology but doesn't alienate clients who prefer direct, personal communication. Your Calendly link serves as a backup, but the initial offer shows your willingness to go the extra mile.

The Power of Texting

I'm also a strong advocate for using text messaging in conjunction with email. Statistics support this: **SMS boasts an open rate of 98%, while email open rates average just 48%**. This is particularly true for busy professionals like lawyers, where time is scarce, and quick communication is essential. By being omnichannel—using both email and SMS—you maximize the chances of securing a meeting.

Here's how I phrase my text:

> "Hi Jane,
>
> Happy Monday! Following up on my email, let me know when you're free for coffee. If you're not against it, how about 3:30 PM today or tomorrow? Alternatively, book in here: [Calendly Link]."

This approach works because it's warm, casual, and to the point, combining the effectiveness of text with the flexibility of scheduling software.

Control Your Calendar

Taking the concept of *"Magician's Choice"* even further, you can control your availability completely when you set up your Calendly or any booking system. You decide which times are available, how long meetings last, and what dates work for you. For instance, I block out weekends and restrict bookings after 6 PM. That way, I create the appearance of high demand while ensuring my work-life balance. For professionals in industries like mine, where most banks close by 4:30 PM, offering availability until 7 PM provides a **2.5-hour competitive edge**. It's about outpacing the competition without burning out.

Tailor your calendar to meet the peak engagement times of your clients. Lawyers, for example, often appreciate early morning slots before court hearings or late afternoons when they're wrapping up their day. By aligning your availability with these prime windows, you're not just meeting expectations—you're exceeding them.

The language you use at every stage also matters. For fellow marketing mavens, I highly recommend experimenting with copy to ensure it feels personal, thoughtful, and aligned with your brand.

Incorporating this blend of human interaction, technology, and strategic timing into your scheduling can elevate your client relationships to a whole new level. You control the outcome without seeming controlling, and your clients feel valued, not managed. This system has not only worked for me with the most demanding clients—like lawyers—but will work for you, too. Just remember: it's all in how you frame the choice.

Assuming you have the paid version of Calendly, once a client selects a date and time slot, my *"Your Finance Review"* booking link will display as follows:

- Company Logo/Branding
- Professional Photo
- Name, Title, Company
- Date, Time & Meeting Duration
- Name of Client
- Email
- Optional Guest Email
- Free Form Message
- Optional Mobile

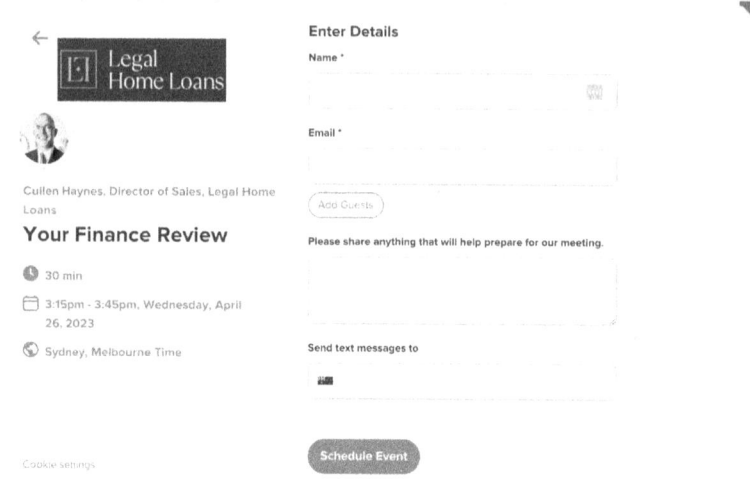

My 'Your Finance Review' Booking Page

Confirmation Page

Even if you choose to use the free version of Calendly initially, that's perfectly fine. I did for the first few months as I adjusted to this new way of working. Once I became comfortable, I upgraded to the paid version, and the additional features far outweighed the cost. For me, it was a game-changer.

I booked more appointments, experienced fewer no-shows, and was able to utilize not just one but three unique and carefully curated calendars.

Paid Version features

- Three Customisable Calendar Links
- Ability to curate journeys, workflows, and templates

- Text Message Automations
- Your Company Branding
- And much more

For context, here are my three current links:

- The first is for finance reviews, allowing legal clients to book a 15-minute consultation.
- The second is for in-person or virtual coffee meetings (the main Calendly link I use on my LinkedIn profile).
- The third is for my LIVE with Cullen Haynes Podcast slots.

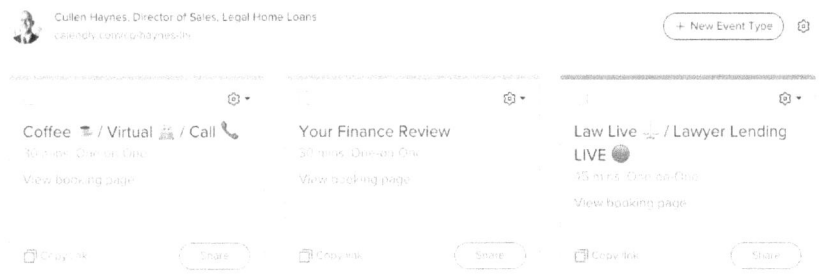

My 3 Calendly Booking Link Options

Upgrading couldn't have come at a better time. I was sending my finance review link for everything, leading to confusion among connections about whether they were receiving a request for an About You form or finance details when they were just meeting for coffee. Similarly, clients booking for the podcast were unsure if the meeting was in person or virtual. This confusion was exacerbated by my packed calendar—something any dedicated 10X advocate would know well.

Learning from Others

Where did I find inspiration for my current calendar journeys? As Tony Robbins says, *"Success leaves clues."* I studied leaders in my field who excelled in their processes. Enter Philippe Doyle Gray.

Observing the Law

Philippe Doyle Gray is a leading barrister at the NSW Bar and a technological savant—an unusual combination in the traditionally conservative field of law. During a coffee meeting with PDG (or rather the booking made just before it), I discovered the true potential of Calendly.

You see, Philippe is an anomaly. As previously mentioned, dear reader, most members of the Bar are quite traditional—they often don't even have a website, let alone a business card. Marketing or any sales activity is generally frowned upon in their world. This is why meeting Philippe was a pivotal moment, a reminder to elevate my own onboarding process from good to great.

It was in this coffee meeting with Philippe that I realized something important. My regular onboarding experience, while functional, lacked that extra edge. I was inspired to build a system that could serve not only my core clients—lawyers—but also elevate any meeting I might have. Below are insights that can help you do the same, whether you're meeting clients, peers, or potential business partners.

The usual tropes are there of course, Name, Email, Mobile, what's unique and different is the location, guest options and talking points.

Location

It all starts with being strategic about where you meet. For me, I have a favourite café—Beanbah—located conveniently near the Supreme Court, a hotspot for lawyers and barristers. This is intentional. By choosing a place that resonates with my clientele, I'm not only creating an atmosphere where they feel at ease, but also tapping into the 'see and be seen' marketing strategy. It's free exposure. People notice you when you're a regular at the places your tribe frequents.

Of course, flexibility is key, so I offer virtual options via Teams or phone calls as well. What's unique about my system is that clients can suggest alternative locations, ensuring the meeting works for them. This adaptability shows respect for their time and preferences, and according to Robert Cialdini's principles of pre-suasion, it starts the interaction off with a high level of inclusivity.

Guest Options

Early on, I underestimated how crucial it is to let people bring others along to meetings. Lawyers often prefer to bring a colleague or partner, and providing that option immediately adds to their comfort. My booking system explicitly welcomes guests, and I even ask how to pronounce their names correctly. This attention to detail makes people feel valued, reinforcing Mark Hughes' wisdom: *"A person's name is the sweetest sound they can hear, so be sure to get it right."*

Talking Points

One of my favourite additions to the system is the 'Talking Points' box. In the past, I'd walk into meetings blind, not knowing what the client wanted to discuss. Now, I receive a full email breakdown when someone books, including key topics they want to cover. This allows me to prepare efficiently, stay sharp, and tailor each conversation to their needs.

This system is really built for speed and for quality.

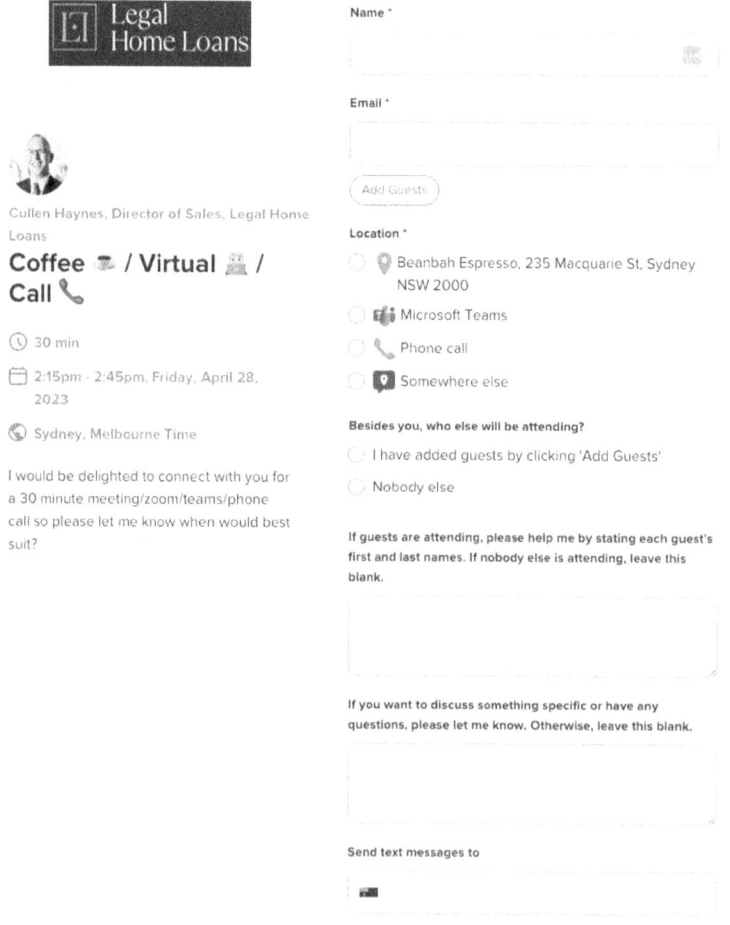

My general booking page Coffee ☕ / Virtual 🧑‍💻 / Call 📞

The Power of Calendly

Calendly has revolutionized the way I organize meetings. The inclusivity and intuitive flow remind me of Apple's seamless design. Clients feel empowered by the 'Magician's Choice,' a psychological term for giving someone multiple options while still guiding them to a preferred outcome. It feels personal and engaging, and as Cialdini might say, this builds rapport before the meeting even starts. Giving system a score of *11/10*; perhaps Spinal Tap's Nigel would agree too!

Transgressing the Law

But remember, as Spiderman's Uncle Ben wisely said, *"With great power comes great responsibility."* When used poorly, tools like Calendly can seem pushy or detached. I can't count how many times I've received a blunt, *"Hey. Book in when works for you. Link below."* Lawyers—like many professionals—are discerning, and a curt invite like that feels transactional. The implied arrogance makes me think, *"Of course, your highness. Let me bend over backward for you."* That's not the energy we want to project.

Believe me dear reader, I've received my fair share and split tested this thousands upon thousands of times. Lawyers would read that and conclude that their own time is not being respected or valued. And as Mary Kay Ash once said, *"Everyone wears an invisible sign around their head saying, 'Make Me Feel Important'"*

Instead, I recommend something like this:

> *"I'd be honoured to meet up and work around your busy schedule. How's 2:30 pm today or tomorrow? Alternatively, feel free to book in when most amenable for you."*

This not only shows respect for their time but positions you as considerate, flexible, and professional.

That's it. Tried, tested, and delivered for you based on real world data from the hardest people to deal with on the planet, lawyers. If they resonate with it, your tribe will too. You can put your faith in this and follow with certainty.

Pro Tip #1 Put Your Calendar on LinkedIn

This cannot be understated. This little hack has brought me countless opportunities. Make it easy, deliberate, and intuitive for clients to book in with you. The easier it is, the more meetings and connections will flow your way.

Pro Tip #2 Block Out Time for Deep Work

While it's great to fill up your calendar with meetings, make sure you block out time for focused work. I'm all for the 10X mindset of filling that calendar up, but you also need time to do the work too. Lawyers respect boundaries and time management, and when they see you've set strategic hours for uninterrupted work, they'll perceive you as an in-demand professional, not someone available 24/7.

Pro Tip #3 Pick a location that resonates

Do some research. Where does your tribe gather? For me, Beanbah near the Supreme Court is perfect because it's central to where my legal clients are based. Every time I'm there, I see familiar faces, and it strengthens my brand presence. It also has the added benefit of free marketing. People see you with a prospect and either say hello or reach out later because they've seen you. To sum it up: See and be seen. Create a system that respects your client's time, makes them feel valued, and sets the stage for a productive, meaningful meeting. Your tribe—and your business—will thank you for it.

Closing Thoughts: Time is Your Greatest Asset

Now, imagine your calendar being as smooth as your favourite coffee—strong, clear, and ready to kick-start your day. Gone are the days of back-and-forth emails, the dreaded double-booking, or the awkward *"Can you do 3pm?"* followed by a four-hour silence. Integrating Calendly has saved me countless hours (and maybe a few grey hairs), allowing me to focus on what truly matters—closing deals, building relationships, and spending time with my family.

But here's the thing: Time, unlike money, is irreplaceable. When you book yourself solid, make sure you're booking the right way. Automate what you can, give your brain space to breathe, and, who knows, you might even find yourself with enough time to enjoy a proper lunch!

Remember, success in business isn't just about how many meetings you have—it's about how efficient and meaningful they are. So go ahead, integrate Calendly, and free yourself from the mundane tasks. You'll thank me later when you're sipping coffee, not stressing over your next appointment.

After all, in the game of law, time isn't just money—it's everything.

Law #23 – Mobilize Your Tribe: Harness the Strength of Networking Groups

The key to power is the ability to form alliances.
— *Robert Greene*

When I first embarked on my LinkedIn journey, I couldn't help but wonder how the heavy hitters were gaining traction within minutes of posting. The same names would pop up as the first to engage, and soon after, the post's reach, engagement, and comments would snowball. What was their secret?

Welcome to the power of networking groups—the secret weapon of the LinkedIn elite. At first glance, it might seem like a shady underground network undermining the integrity of the platform. But in reality, networking groups are a strategic tool that allows connections to support each other's content, ultimately helping everyone succeed.

Setting the Table: A LinkedIn Dinner Analogy

Let's break down LinkedIn networking in terms of a dinner party. Your table is set. You've prepared great content (your cutlery) and have a strategy (your menu) to guide the timing of your posts. Your Calendly link (the waiter) is ready to take orders. The presentation—complete with an engaging title, hashtags, and background photo—looks flawless. But there's one problem: you're missing the main course. No matter how well-prepared you are, if people don't see your content, you'll struggle to build momentum.

Perhaps the analogy is off. The real issue is that your tribe is wandering the streets outside your restaurant, unaware of your delicious offering and thus not booking in to make a reservation.

This is where Telegram comes in—it's the door to your restaurant, providing the algorithmic boost your posts need to get noticed.

For those unfamiliar, Telegram is a cross-platform, encrypted messaging service that delivers messages faster than any other app. As it says on its website, today's Telegram is a cross-platform, encrypted messaging service that delivers messages faster than any other app. There are no limits on the size of media or chats, making it the ideal platform for networking groups.

When I first dialled in on the power of networking groups, it was via my good friend who introduced me to them via the LinkedIn messenger feature itself. While quite novel, the constant messaging clogged my inbox, not to mention the speed was greatly degraded, the more messages were being put into the chat.

When my friend suddenly deleted the group one day, I was scratching my head and albeit a tad concerned. LinkedIn must have cracked down on these groups I rationalised. Not the case at all. In fact, the head honchos at LinkedIn support thriving networking groups that promote the support of others content. What they don't like, is the utilisation of giant faceless Super Pods, where there are over 500-1,000 people, mostly from overseas, completely unrelated to your field (that you don't know) engaging on your content. Not only is this vanity for vanity's sake, but the consequence is also unrelated eyeballs on your content and stricter shadow banning and downgrading of future content by the powers that be. Steer clear of these groups, as they may seem like a quick way to build a tribe, but they often lead to shadow banning or downgrading of your content.

While I was worrying about my friend facing LinkedIn jail, he was actually ahead of the curve, moving everyone over to Telegram. And it couldn't have come at a more apt time. With the mass exodus from platforms like WhatsApp and Meta, Telegram is fast becoming the application of choice for those wanting to keep up with friends, family, and connections.

For those die-hard LinkedIn Law Benders, like you and me, Telegram helps facilitate content support among a close-knit tribe of influencers and professionals. The only rule? **Givers gain**—the more you give, the more you get in return.

LinkedIn Judgement – The Algorithm: Engagement is Key

The algorithm will always give credence to content that has more engagement in the first 20 minutes. So, the idea of a winning networking group is you post your content, copy the link, and drop it into the group, while ensuring you also engage with your friends' content. Your network will see post and engage as soon as they can, which gives your content a fantastic push in the feed. Think of it as a radar beacon for your close connections, that can easily find it and support you, rather than having to trawl your account or have the random burst of data that they see you in the feed. I find it a much better, and more efficient way of supporting those you care about.

So, if you're starting out and thinking, I don't have a tribe of like-minded winners like yourself yet (trust me, it will happen) come together at your company or get 5-10 close friends/colleagues to start a support group on Telegram with you. You should set the expectation that you will support each other equally and it would be preferable to select those who have like-minded values and have the BHAG of wanting to take their content to the next level. It's a thriving, symbiotic group where you both like and comment on each other's stuff to show that you care and get that content boosted,

Pro Tip #1 – Givers Gain

While there are no strict rules in networking groups, but one principle stands above all, **givers gain.** The more you give to others in the group—through liking, commenting, and sharing—the more support you'll receive in return.

Before copying your own content into the group, go back over the last 24 hours and engage: like, comment and share all your colleagues' posts. This way, when you drop yours, they'll be quick to reciprocate.

No one appreciates freeloaders or leeches, and you'll soon find yourself with little engagement or removed from the group entirely. (I've seen it happen many a time).

Observing the Law

When I joined a group of 10 finance and business professionals over four years ago, I was immediately struck by the open and supportive culture that emerged organically within the group. The group thrived on flexibility and mutual encouragement, without rigid rules or formalities. There were no strict posting schedules (you must post at 8am), no restrictions on which social media platforms to use, and no specific content limitations. Whether it was LinkedIn, TikTok, or another platform, we could post how, when, and what we wanted, as often as we wanted.

The group followed two key principles that every member was encouraged to follow:

- **Any content, any time!**
- **Givers gain – Like. Share. Comment.**

The last part was especially vital. Before posting your own content, the culture dictated that you engage with others by liking and commenting on posts from the past 24 hours. Adding thoughtful insights in your comments fostered stronger connections and deeper engagement, creating an ecosystem where everyone supported one another's growth.

By removing unnecessary restrictions and fostering a genuine *"give-first"* mentality, the group thrived, demonstrating the power of reciprocal support and how networking groups, when managed well, can amplify everyone's success.

Pro Tip #2 – Read Before You Comment

Don't just drop a generic "Great post!" without first reading it. In my early Group days, I'm such a high energy person I would like, share, and comment in a positive way *"Hey Hayley, inspirational post, love your work"* not realising that the post in questions was a tribute to the author's recently deceased dog. #Cringe #FacePalm #BombasticSideeye —lesson learned. Note to self from then on, do not in your haste comment before reading or viewing the image in detail. Take your time. Go slow to go fast. It will pay off in spades when you engage with insights.

Transgressing the Law

A broking colleague of mine once created a Telegram group with the best of intentions, but soon, it became clear the group was moving in the wrong direction. At first, it was a collaborative culture where everyone was able to share whatever and whenever they wanted and engaged whenever they had time. Then the nefarious influence of control began to raise its ugly head when a few members from other networking groups joined and wanted to introduce some rules that apparently *"Elite Groups"* follow. I'll never forget the day when it was announced that we'd be moving to a few guidelines that everyone had to follow, and if you didn't you either liked it—or left. It was that simple.

- LinkedIn only – We don't want any posts from other platforms thank you!
- 8am & 5pm only – We'd appreciate you didn't post in between the allotted times
- You MUST like every post in the group, no exceptions
- 1 Post MAX per day – It's only fair that you honour this rule, as it's too much for people to support 3-5 posts from any other person.

That was the beginning of the end for me, because not only did it stymie any sort of creative and supportive culture, but they had also left at that point it encouraged bullying and other types of anti-social behaviour.

I remember one gentleman who I will not name and shame but had a problem with liking every single person's post and made a point to call out (in detail) individual members content and things he didn't like. I remember his mic drop comment at the end *"If you don't like the way I do things, I'll just take my 'Like' elsewhere."*

What's more is that the head of the group, my broking colleague didn't call out the behaviour, he just liked it and said he agreed.

That was my last day in that particular group, as soon as I heard that, I was like *"Bye Felicia. Bye."*

I heard that group eventually imploded and was closed shortly after. I'm glad I saw the writing on the wall.

Pro Tip #3 – Quality over Quantity

On the above note, outside of your company go for quality over quantity when it comes to networking groups. In my initiate LinkedIn days, I experimented with being a part of multiple groups at once and felt very discouraged as not only did it take an enormous amount of time to support multiple people's posts in each group, but I also found I either didn't like the culture, case in point above, or didn't resonate with the collective content strategy or vibe of the individual's actual content.

I stand by my decision in 2019, best to find a quality collection of people to support rather than a volume strategy where you're supporting many and spreading yourself and your energy thin. Better to minor in major than major in minor.

Pro Tip #4 – You're So Vain: Avoid Vanity Metrics

Avoid spammy groups that shoot your likes up to 400 to 500 in a matter of 1 hour. These superficial engagements might look impressive, but they won't help you build meaningful connections or business opportunities. LinkedIn actively penalizes users who engage in spammy groups. The comments are usually disingenuous, the engagement very spammy and worst still is the powers that be will limit the reach of your audience albeit at the very least will be skewed by the foreign engagers who will never ever buy your product. The engagement you're getting won't translate into meaningful connections or opportunities.

I often laugh when I see known users who engage in these tactics forget to post as their post gets 2-3 likes then an hour later up to 400! It's blatantly obvious that they forgot to post in their network and voila, when they do, likes and comments soar.

What's telling is that overall engagement is low. What that communicates to me is that while they are receiving quantity on their post, they're not receiving the quality engagement that further boosts eyeballs on your content. Which in my judgement defeats the purpose of LinkedIn.

Remember, the purpose of LinkedIn is simple: find your tribe, add value to your tribe, and be paid in accordance with the value you bring. *"You get paid based on the value you bring to the marketplace, not time"* - Jim Rohn. So do not fall into the trap or pay for the services of LinkedIn gurus who have exceedingly high likes and comments and promise the same in return. It's similar to paying for Instagram followers, high follower and like count yes, low return. True success comes from building genuine relationships and offering consistent value.

You have been warned!

Remember this philosophy that bears repeating. Givers gain & watch your engagement soar.

Closing Thoughts: Your Network, Your Power

In the end, success is rarely a solo endeavour. It's the result of a carefully cultivated network—a tribe of people who lift each other up, push each other forward, and celebrate each other's wins. The world is full of noise, but in the right networking group, you find clarity, strength, and support.

As you mobilize your tribe, remember that the true power lies in how you contribute, not just what you gain. Give with authenticity, engage with purpose, and watch the ripple effect take hold. The more you invest in your network, the more your network will invest in you.

So, don't just sit on the sidelines of your tribe—get in the game, take the lead and build something remarkable with the people around you. The strength of your network is a direct reflection of the strength of your influence.

And that, my friend, is a law worth following.

Bonus Law - The Ultimate Goal: Take Your Online Interactions Offline

The real world is a lot messier and more complicated than the online world. Nothing beats face-to-face interaction.
— Ryan Holiday

As we wrap up this journey through the laws of LinkedIn, there's one more concept I want to spotlight—a *bonus law* that ties everything together. This principle has been woven throughout the chapters, but it deserves its own moment of glory. It's an idea that has been core to my approach on LinkedIn: **The goal of LinkedIn is to take your online interactions into the real world.**

While each law we've explored is a tool to help you build influence, engagement, and connections, this is the ultimate goal. All the likes, comments, and shares are just the beginning. The real magic happens when you take those digital connections offline—into phone calls, Zoom meetings, coffees, collaborations, and partnerships that lead to real-world impact.

David Gale, a close friend and renowned family law expert who shares his insights on both LinkedIn and TikTok, loved this message when he read the draft of the book and emphasized just how essential it is. He said, *"I love the tips in this book, both those that I also use and endorse (esp. Calendly—omg, the best app ever!) and those (many) that you have brought to my attention! But this message about taking the online offline is the one that resonates deeply. It deserves more prominence because, let's face it, if LinkedIn interactions don't convert to real-world engagement, what's the point?"*

David's point couldn't be clearer: LinkedIn is like a professional networking event that never ends. You can choose to engage superficially, handing out digital business cards and collecting connections, or you can dive deeper, creating meaningful conversations that lead to real opportunities. Much like at an in-person event, it's the depth of the interaction—not just the quantity—that leads to lasting relationships.

And here's where David nailed it: *"Negative content is easier to make and gets more attention. But what I've always liked about your content is its positivity. It takes real skill and authenticity to post positive content that's not just virtue-signalling—and you do that exceptionally well."*

This insight is essential. LinkedIn is flooded with negativity, hot takes, and controversy designed to grab attention. But for those of us looking to build meaningful, lasting connections, its positivity, authenticity, and real value that stand out. When you combine that with the intent to take those connections offline, you become unstoppable.

Taking the Online Offline – The True Power of LinkedIn

In the early days of Legal Home Loans, we had what we thought was a game-changing idea—the **LHL Running Club**. The goal? To take our online LinkedIn connections and turn them into real-world relationships by inviting members of the legal community to meet, run, and connect in a healthy, safe environment. It was all about transforming those digital engagements into genuine connections.

Did the idea blow up like we'd hoped? Not quite. In fact, on our debut run, only Olympian and law firm owner Hayder Shkara laced up with us (big shout out to Hayder!). But here's the thing—even though the turnout was small, the idea was sound. The mission of taking the online offline was there.

I still chuckle when I look at our promo photo—AJ is mid-way through ripping off his tie like he's about to clock out of corporate life, and I'm halfway out of my business shirt, one foot already in a running shoe, the other still in work mode. It's a fun reminder that even when things don't go according to plan, you should keep experimenting. As Wayne Dyer famously said, *"There's no such thing as failure, only results."* Every attempt gets you closer to the right one.

And that's the core of LinkedIn—it's not just about racking up connections but transforming those connections into real, meaningful interactions in the real world. Keep testing, keep pushing, and remember, the only true failure is in not trying.

The LHL Running Club | July 2018

Closing Thoughts: Make the Real Connection

So, here's the final takeaway: everything you've learned in this book, every law, every strategy—it all leads to this. **Take your online interactions offline.** It's easy to stay in the comfort of LinkedIn's digital space, but the real growth happens when you take action in the real world.

Whether it's setting up that meeting through Calendly (yes, David—an amazing tool!), having a coffee chat, or starting a business relationship—don't let your interactions live and die online. Use LinkedIn to open doors, but step through those doors in the real world.

The positivity you share, the authenticity you bring, and the value you offer will shine brightest when you make that real-world connection. As you go forward, keep this final law in mind. It could be the one that turns your LinkedIn presence from a powerful tool into a life-changing platform for real-world success.

EPILOGUE

Don't wish it was easier wish you were better. Don't wish for less problems wish for more skills. Don't wish for less challenge wish for more wisdom.
— *Jim Rohn*

As I sit here, reflecting on how best to close this book and my journey on LinkedIn so far, one story comes to mind—the story of *The Chinese Farmer*. It perfectly encapsulates not just the essence of this book—but also the unpredictability of life on LinkedIn and beyond.

We often expect immediate results, but in reality, the most meaningful outcomes take time to reveal themselves. The best things that have happened to me at LHL stemmed from encounters and opportunities that weren't immediately obvious. Let me illustrate this with the story of The Chinese Farmer, a lesson in patience and perspective:

> *A farmer and his son had a beloved horse that helped them earn their living. One day, the horse ran away. The neighbours came by and exclaimed, "Your horse ran away? What terrible luck!" The farmer calmly replied, "Maybe so, maybe not."*
>
> *A few days later, the horse returned, bringing with it several wild horses. The neighbours rushed over, "Your horse has come back, and with more! What great luck!" The farmer simply said, "Maybe so, maybe not."*
>
> *Later, while trying to break in one of the wild horses, the farmer's son was thrown and broke his leg. The neighbours,*

ever concerned, said, "Your son broke his leg. What terrible luck!" The farmer, as always, replied, "Maybe so, maybe not."

A few weeks later, soldiers came to town, recruiting all the young men for the army. Because of his broken leg, the farmer's son was spared. The neighbours rejoiced, "Your son was spared! What tremendous luck!" And, true to form, the farmer said, "Maybe so, maybe not. We'll see."

The Moral of the Story?

It's hard to judge events as inherently good or bad in the moment. Life—and LinkedIn—are full of twists, and only time reveals the true impact of our actions. So, when you're building your presence, cultivating relationships, or chasing goals, remember this: the results you're seeking might not arrive tomorrow, next week, or even next year. But if you keep showing up, investing in yourself, and giving back to your community, you'll eventually see the bigger picture. In time, your efforts will bear fruit in unexpected ways.

Will this book guarantee immediate success on LinkedIn? Maybe, maybe not. But much like the story of the Chinese Farmer, the seeds you plant today may bear fruit in ways you can't yet foresee. Keep an open mind, embrace the journey, and in time, the true value of your efforts will reveal itself. Only then, looking back, will you truly understand the impact of the actions you've taken.

Some Final Thoughts to Help You Win Big on LinkedIn

As we wrap up this book, I want to leave you with some actionable insights and timeless strategies to keep growing and thriving on LinkedIn. These tips have served me well, and I'm confident these strategies will fuel your LinkedIn growth, as long as you implement them consistently.

Take the Online, Offline

The goal of LinkedIn is to take your online interactions into the real world. Don't dismiss coffee meetings just because the person doesn't immediately appear to fit your 'tribe.' Everyone you meet has a network of 120+ people— One of those connections might lead to a pivotal opportunity to expanding your influence. Lesson: take every coffee, you never know where it might lead.

Share Your Routine – Health is Wealth

Your LinkedIn strategy should also include a healthy body and mind. Establish routines not only for content creation but also for your well-being. Share your health regimen or daily habits with your network— whether it's morning runs, yoga, or evening gym sessions. You might find others who share similar habits and want to connect in person.

The Best Time to Post

In my experience, 7:30 AM is the sweet spot for LinkedIn posts. It's early enough to catch people on their commute but not too late that they've already started their day. After testing various posting times to see which performed better, 6:30 AM felt too early and 9 AM too late. Use this as a guide, but remember, consistency is key

20/100 My Daily Goal

I set myself the goal of 20 new connections a day and 100 messages. The messages could be anything—comments, promotions, or birthday wishes. It's essential to not only grow your network but also nurture and engage with your existing connections.

You Reap More Than What You Sow

We often hear "you reap what you sow," but in my experience, you reap more than you sow—positively or negatively. Focus on your daily efforts rather than the outcomes. If you put in consistent, extraordinary effort, the results will come. A great resource that expands on this idea is Hal Elrod's *Miracle Equation*, where he explains that *"Extraordinary Effort + Unwavering Belief = Miracles."*

Trolls Are Your Best Friend

While it's never nice to get trolled online, know that the algorithm on LinkedIn and other platforms like YouTube cannot distinguish between positive and negative engagement. It's all the same. Any engagement adds to the eyeballs on your content. In the rare occasion I see a pointed message or someone trying to gaslight me, I simply write *"Thank you so much."* And as Grant Cardone once said, *"I need more haters, the old ones are starting to like me"*

Don't Panic When Followers Drop

Every now and then, you'll lose a couple of followers after posting. Don't sweat it. For every 1-2 followers you lose, you'll gain 5-10 in the long run. Remember, those that have unfollowed you were not the tribe members you want following you anyway. I've had lawyers and clients unfollow me, only to return when they needed my services.

Repurpose Your Content

Don't limit yourself to one platform. If you've created a killer video for LinkedIn, share it across TikTok, Instagram, and YouTube. Tailor it slightly to fit each platform but remember—people just need to *see* you. For TikTok, shorten your video to under 60 seconds; for Instagram, optimize for visual impact with captions. The more omnipresent you are, the more you'll expand your influence.

LinkedIn Live, Streamyard & Podcasting

As discussed earlier, LinkedIn Live utilising Streamyard is a great way to broaden your influence. I feel it's made for interviews so when you get access, invite your clients on, keep it to 20-35 mins and once uploaded, depending on the package you've ordered through Streamyard, it's beamed live and uploaded to Facebook, LinkedIn, YouTube, Instagram,

X, Twitch etc. After it's uploaded, you can rip the audio then upload to your podcast straight after.

Again, check out StreamYard: **https://streamyard.com/pal/d/5229683975913472**

Be Present in Industry Publications

Know where your tribe hangs out and subscribe to their go-to publications. For our business, I've found, *Lawyers Weekly*, run by *Momentum Media* (The Sydney Morning Herald for over 100,000 legal professionals) has made it so much easier for my connection and congratulatory game. As when I get an article in my inbox and see someone featured, I'll add that person, congratulate them, and invite for coffee. Very powerful way to build connections.

Comment on Everyone's Content

Make it a priority to respond to every comment on your posts. As I have undiagnosed ADHD and OCD, it's a politeness thing for me that I get back to everyone who has engaged by commenting back and thanking them, as they've boosted my content, only fair I let them know they've been seen. Do not outsource this—it's best to keep it in-house and preserve the authenticity of your voice.

See and Be Seen

When you go for a coffee meeting, pick a visible spot where your tribe is likely to pass by. It's a strategy I learned during my time at

Macquarie—serendipitous encounters can lead to new opportunities. And don't forget, breakfast meetings in the right places can work wonders for your network.

Engage with insights!

When you comment on another's posts or even your own followers' comments, be sure to engage with insights. Compliment in a meaningful way *"Cogent insights here Oliver, never looked at it that way"* or ask a question *"Interesting Lucy, what else do you think might happen?"* That way you're keeping the content fresh and the conversation going with not only the person you're engaging on, but others who are passing by and connected with that person too.

The algorithm also likes it if you engage using some of the verbiage that the person used too.

Don't Edit Your Post in first 10 Minutes

This seems to be an unwritten rule I've been following for some time. **Editing your post immediately after publishing can hinder its engagement.** When you post something on LinkedIn, it takes time for the algorithm to start promoting it in users' feeds. If you edit your post too soon, you may disrupt this process. I've learned this the hard way when posts flopped after I edited them too quickly.

Research suggests that **social media engagement often follows the *"10-minute rule,"*** where posts that gain early interactions (likes, comments, shares) within the first 10 minutes tend to perform better in the long run. A study from *Buffer* found that posts that received a significant amount of engagement shortly after being published continued to be favoured by algorithms across various platforms. This early momentum can lead to increased visibility and further engagement as the post circulates through the network.

Moreover, **editing a post shortly after publishing can lead to confusion among initial viewers.** If someone engages with a post only to find that the content has changed or is inconsistent, they might feel disoriented or less likely to engage in the future. Keeping your original post intact for at least 10 minutes allows the audience to interact with your content as intended, maximizing its impact and fostering genuine engagement.

Navigating Algorithm Shifts

It's natural to feel frustrated when your post engagement dips, but remember: LinkedIn's algorithm is always evolving. One-week polls might drive massive interactions, and the next, it's videos taking centre stage. A recent LinkedIn study showed that video content has been receiving a major boost in 2024, aligning with broader social media trends favoring video for engagement. However, this could change quickly, as algorithms periodically shift focus between formats like single images, text posts, or even carousels.

I experienced this firsthand in mid-2023, when polls were incredibly popular, generating thousands of views. But by the end of the year, their effectiveness waned, and I noticed video content outperforming everything else. When the algorithm changed, I felt the pinch, but instead of sticking to what worked before, I diversified my content—testing image posts, video snippets, and carousels—which helped maintain consistent engagement. The takeaway? Stay flexible. By adapting to the algorithm's shifts and not putting all your eggs in one content basket, you can continue to drive engagement and reach your audience.

So, don't get discouraged when the algorithm changes—see it as an opportunity to experiment and refine your strategy.

Respond to Comments in the First Hour

When you post and receive engagement, be sure to respond within the first hour. **Timely responses to comments can significantly boost your post's visibility and engagement.** The LinkedIn algorithm favours posts that generate interaction shortly after being published, and your active participation in the conversation can help maintain that momentum.

Research indicates that **engaging with your audience quickly can increase the likelihood of further interactions.** According to a study by *HubSpot*, posts that receive replies within the first hour can see a **boost in their overall reach by up to 50%** compared to those that do not receive timely responses.

This is due to the way social media algorithms prioritize content that demonstrates active engagement and conversation.

Engage with 7 (Minimum 3 Posts) after Posting

Engaging with other users' content—whether through comments, likes, or shares—can significantly impact your own post's performance. When you interact with others, you signal to the LinkedIn algorithm that you are an active participant in the platform. As a result, your posts are more likely to be shown to a broader audience, which can lead to increased engagement and reach.

Research from LinkedIn itself supports this strategy: posts by users who engage with other content tend to see **higher visibility and interaction rates.** A study by *Sprout Social* found that engagement can lead to a **potential increase of up to 33% in post interactions**. This occurs because your engagement can prompt others to check out your profile and posts, creating a reciprocal relationship where they are more likely to engage with your content in return.

Moreover, by actively engaging with the posts of others, you are nurturing your professional relationships and expanding your network. Engaging with your connections not only helps maintain relationships but also keeps you informed about their activities, interests, and insights. This knowledge can be invaluable when crafting future content that resonates with your audience.

Reach Within the First 8 Hours is Based on Engagement in the First 90 Minutes

One of the key insights about LinkedIn's algorithm is that **the reach of your post in the first 8 hours** is largely determined by the **engagement it receives in the first 90 minutes**. This engagement window plays a crucial role in how widely your post is shown to others on the platform.

LinkedIn's algorithm favours content that generates early interactions—likes, comments, shares—because it interprets this as a signal that the post is valuable and engaging. The more engagement your post garners in that critical first 90-minute window, the more the algorithm boosts its visibility to a larger audience. This early engagement kicks your post into high gear, driving more visibility throughout the day.

According to research by LinkedIn, posts that gain **higher initial engagement** are more likely to trend and continue being surfaced in newsfeeds throughout the day. **LinkedIn Insider data** suggests that the algorithm analyses early responses to determine how much to promote the post across users' feeds, with initial engagement correlating to an **up to 20% increase in reach**.

To take advantage of this, it's important to strategically encourage interactions as soon as you post. Consider notifying key connections, using engaging hooks, or asking questions that prompt quick responses. It's also essential to monitor your post during this window and actively respond to comments and likes to maintain momentum.

ACKNOWLEDGMENTS

First and foremost, I want to express my deepest gratitude to my loving wife, Emmy. Your unwavering support and encouragement have been the foundation upon which this work was built. You've believed in me even when I doubted myself, and your love fuels my ambition every day. I love you always and all ways.

To my family, thank you for your endless patience and understanding. Your sacrifices and encouragement have shaped me into the person I am today. I am eternally grateful for your presence in my life.

I'd like to extend a special thank you to my friends and business partners, Andrew and Aylin. Our years of collaboration at Legal Home Loans have been rewarding, and I am excited about the journey ahead as we continue to build together. Your insights and camaraderie have made this journey successful and enjoyable.

Thanks to our legal and accounting clients for your unwavering support over the years. Your trust and partnership have enriched my life and inspired this work. I am honoured to serve you. Your success fuels my passion, and I cannot wait to witness the remarkable milestones you will reach.

I also want to express my gratitude to everyone who picks up this book. May it inspire you to pursue your goals, foster connections, and embark on your own journey of growth and achievement.

A special thanks to my publisher, Balboa Press (a division of Hay House), for making this book a reality. Your team has been invaluable in bringing this project to life.

Thank you to Microsoft and LinkedIn for creating platforms that have empowered professionals worldwide, including myself, to connect, share, and grow. Your tools have been instrumental in bringing *The Laws of LinkedIn* to life.

And to all my valued LinkedIn connections, thank you for inspiring me every day. Your interactions demonstrate the power of community and meaningful relationships.

This book is a testament to the incredible people in my life, and I look forward to what the future holds for all of us.

Thank you all for being a part of this journey.

Cullen P. Haynes

www.ingramcontent.com/pod-product-compliance
Lightning Source LLC
Chambersburg PA
CBHW071352210526
45465CB00001B/61